PROPHETISM IN GHANA

Prof. (Emiritus) C.G. Baëta, OBE, GM, FGA.
BA, BD, PhD (Lond), Hon DD (Tokyo), Hon LLD (Hope), Hon D Theol (Humboldt), Hon Th.D. (Debrecen), D Litt (Legon).

PROPHETISM IN GHANA
A Study of Some 'Spiritual' Churches

C.G. BAËTA

First Published by SCM Press

© 2004, 1962 C.G. Baëta
Reprint by Africa Christian Press

All rights reserved. No part of this book may be reproduced, stored in a retrival system, or transmitted, in any form or by any means, electronic, mechanical, photocopying, recording, or otherwise, without the written permission of Africa Christian Press.

Cover Design & Typesetting
Francis K. N. Nunoo

Africa Christian Press
Achimota, Ghana

ISBN: 9964-87-802-8

This reprint to the glory of God
and dedicated to the memory of the late
Prof. (Emiritus) C. G. Baëta
who was called home to glory in 1994

CONTENTS

	Brief Biography of the Author	viii
	Foreword	ix
	Preface	xvii
1	Introduction	1
2	The Church of the Twelve Apostles	8
3	The Musama Disco Christo Church	26
4	Memeneda Gyidifo (The Saviour Church)	65
5	Apostolowo Fe Dedefia Habobo (The Apostolic Revelation Society)	72
6	Etodome Nyanyuie-Presbiteria Hame Gbedoda Kple Doyo-Habobo (The Prayer and Healing Group of the Evangelical Presbyterian Church at Etodome)	89
7	Other Groups:	
	The African Faith Tabernacle Congregation	107
	The Eternal Sacred Order of Cherubim and Seraphim Society	109
	The Church of the Lord (Aladura)	113
8	Conclusion	121
	Select Bibliography	140
	Appendices	142

BRIEF BIOGRAPHY OF THE AUTHOR

The Late Rev. Prof. Emeritus Christian Gonçalves Baëta was born on 23rd May, 1908 and died on 29th December, 1994. He was a man dedicated to his calling as a Christian. He was a man of many parts. In his early years he was an examiner in Ewe for the London Matriculation and Cambridge School Certificate Examinations, and also an examiner for the Gold Coast Teacher's Efficiency Bar Examinations. In addition he worked as an Ewe announcer for Accra Radio ZOY during the Vichy crisis in Togoland.

In 1945/46, the Rev. Prof. Baëta was appointed the Principal of the Ewe Presby Church Theological College at Ho. He was also a Synod Clerk of his church. In 1946, he was elected Legislative Council Member for the Eastern Province of the Gold Coast.

Later, he was appointed Senior Lecturer in Theology at the University College (later the University of Ghana), Legon. He became Professor and Head of the Department of the Study of Religions till his retirement in 1971.

He obtained his Ph.D. degree from the University of London, and was awarded several honorary doctorate degrees from universities the world over: DD (Tokyo), LLD (Hope), D Theol (Humboldt), Th. D (Debrecen), D Litt (Legon)

Rev. Prof. Baëta served at the University of Ghana for a period of 22 years as Lecturer, Professor, Protestant Chaplain, Master of Legon Hall, Dean of the Faculty of Arts and Pro-Vice Chancellor. He held visiting professorships at Union Theological Seminary in New York, USA; at the Selly Oak Colleges in Birmingham, UK., and the Ruhr-Universität in Bochum, Germany where he taught his courses in German.

He was a fellow of the Ghana Academy of Arts and Science till his death. He was president of the Academy for two consecutive terms, 1991 and 1992. He was the last chairman of the International Missionary Council and superintended the integration of the Council into the World Council of Churches in 1961.

In recognition of his many achievements, Prof. Baëta was awarded the OBE by Her Majesty, Queen Elizabeth of Great Britain and the Commonwealth, and the Grand Medal of Ghana. He was the first to be awarded the title, Professor Emeritus, by the University of Ghana, Legon

FOREWORD

The Prophetic in Christian G. Baëta's *Prophetism In Ghana*

It is more than three decades now since Christian Gonçalves Baëta's widely acknowledged seminal 'study of some "Spiritual" Churches' in Ghana was published. In an excellent review of the book, Harold W. Turner, himself a leading scholar in the field of African Christian independency, noted that 'there is no other work of such substance by an African scholar among the growing literature on African prophet movements and independent churches.' C.G. Baëta, Turner continued, 'has given us the first extended work on these phenomena in this whole area.'[1] Professor Baëta, a former chair and professor emeritus of the Department for the Study of Religions at the University of Ghana was called home to glory a decade ago. This new foreword to his *Prophetism in Ghana*, which is written at the request of his children, is for me a rare privilege to affirm the work of one whose achievements as an academic, ecumenist, preacher and minister of the gospel I came to admire even before I met him.

During my days as a student at Trinity Theological Seminary, Legon, Ghana in the early 1980s, I served as an intern at the Accra Ridge Church where the old man also worshipped. As seminarians, we often invited this retired doyen of independent African Christianity to come and give us lectures on various subjects of interest related to his field. His last lecture to us was on the 'Spiritual churches and witchcraft.' Our paths crossed several times after these meetings, including once at a 1994 conference of the African Theological Fellowship in Accra, Ghana.[2] As chairperson of one of the plenary sessions, Professor Baëta, without any prepared manuscript, offered a brilliant exposé on current developments within Christianity in Africa. It was always a rewarding and enriching experience listening to Professor Baëta on African Christianity even during his retirement years, and I have always wondered what he would have thought of recent developments.

This foreword, therefore, affords me the rare opportunity to revisit some of Baëta's conclusions in the light of recent innovations and developments in African Christian independency. In spite of the seismic changes that have occurred within the field, Baëta's study remains one of the most informative, insightful, and authoritative academic sources on Christian religious innovation in twentieth-century Africa in general, and Ghana in particular. The findings of *Prophetism in Ghana* served as a point of departure for my own work on current developments within Ghanaian Christianity from the last quarter of the twentieth century.[3] The African independent churches (AICs) in their various manifestations across the continent, whether as Spiritual, Zionist, or Aladura churches, remain the most intensely studied streams of indigenous Christianity in Africa since the turn of the last century. To this end, one of the leading players in the academic field of African Christianity, the late Professor

FOREWORD

Adrian Hastings of Leeds University, observed that scholars looking for interesting research topics in the field of African religion at the height of the popularity of the AICs in the 1960s, could hardly fail to be attracted by one of the almost innumerable new churches springing into vibrant existence in Africa. 'African Christianity,' according to Hastings, suddenly became 'a popular subject indeed but almost entirely in terms of the independent churches.'[4]

C.G. Baëta was one of the pace setters in that field of study, and his works will remain important reference points for all those seeking an understanding of Christian religious innovation on the continent of Africa. Indeed, *Prophetism in Ghana* has served as an invaluable source of reference for most of the studies on AICs including publications that are not directly related to Ghana. Professor Baëta's work thus stands as a great tribute to his memory as a 'prophet' in his own right. His 'prophetic' approach to the study of indigenous Christianity in Africa makes the reissue of the book at this time, very appropriate. In spite of some scathing criticisms of what he sometimes saw as a simplistic and shallow understanding of the Christian scriptures and theologies of the Spiritual churches, Baëta was on the whole sympathetic to the cause of the movements he studied. He did recognize in the Spiritual churches a major step forward in an attempt to make Christianity speak to African situations in more relevant ways than the historic mission churches were doing at the time. The encounter between Christianity in Africa and the African indigenous religions with their ardent beliefs in myriads of supernatural powers for health, protection, and survival, produced profound results with many Africans clandestinely tapping from both resources in their quests for salvation. Baëta referred to the schizophrenic phenomenon of being a church member during the day while seeking protection from traditional shrines at night as 'braces and belt' Christianity, an attitude of religious syncretism quite common in Africa.[5] The search for practical salvation, which he identified as a key source of attraction into the Spiritual churches lives on in the modern manifestations of these churches.

Prophetism in Ghana recognized in some of the Spiritual churches an attempt to put an end to such hypocritical Christianity in spite of any shortcomings they may have had. Based on his reading of 1 Thessalonians 1:9, Baëta considered the members of the Spiritual churches he observed at the time as representing African Christians who, like the Thessalonians of St. Paul's day, had turned 'away from these traditional resources of supernatural succour in order that help may be sought, for the same purposes, from the God of the Christian evangel.' This conversion process, according to Baëta, was 'the greatest positive step' that the Spiritual churches took. In his own words:

> *The 'spiritual churches' indeed have a very strong conviction that at long last the passage has been made from error to truth, from the wrong path to the right one, from darkness to light; and that, because this is so, the newly-found resource of helpful power cannot fail.*[6]

FOREWORD

Major changes have occurred in the field of African Christianity since the height of the revivals initiated by the AICs at the turn of the twentieth century. Some of the phenomena and religious orientations that Baëta identified have remained resilient in the face of these changes. For example, he saw in the Spiritual churches what he described then as 'a prodigious struggle to prove the reality of spiritual things in general and the biblical promises in particular.'[7]

This idiom of 'power' from the Holy Spirit identified in *Prophetism in Ghana* as a key underlying theme of independent indigenous spirituality has also resurfaced as a critical aspect of the religion of the modern progenies of Ghana's Spiritual churches. These are the movements that Ogbu Kalu aptly refers to as the 'third response' to the missionary enterprise in Africa following the nationalist churches of the late nineteenth century and then the AICs.[8] The new independent churches in question are popularly referred to in Ghana as the Charismatic Ministries (CMs) and possess a different physical outlook from the classical AICs. They are made up of a relatively more educated and younger following than the Spiritual churches and also make use of more modern instruments of Christian expression including an extensive use of media technologies. The CMs have dropped the use of uniforms and such paraphernalia as the African gourd rattle, which the Church of the Twelve Apostles, one of those studied by Baëta, believed was enchanted with the presence of the Spirit. Even though the CMs may be physically different from the older AICs, they are both African-initiated movements and, as Andrew Walls explains, the CMs share with their forebears 'a quest for the demonstrable presence of the Holy Spirit and a direct address to the problems and frustrations of modern African urban life.'[9] In other words some appreciation of the spirituality of the Spiritual churches may be needed for a fuller understanding of modern Ghanaian charismatic Christianity, and Baëta's work provides the key background text for this endeavor.

The very designation of 'Spiritual churches' that Baëta used for Ghana's version of the older AICs, against such other terms and expressions as 'separatist,' 'messianic' or 'syncretist' cults, underscored their pneumatic orientation. Against the backdrop of accusations that the incorporation of elements from traditional African religious rituals into AIC spiritualities represented aberrations of the Christian church and of the gospel of Jesus Christ, Baëta became one of those scholars who firmly and sincerely believed in the decidedly Christian orientation of these churches. The new Charismatic churches are some of the ardent critics of the Spiritual churches because of the perceived proximity of their healing rituals to those found in the African traditional shrines. Yet in several respects, the theologies of the two movements, especially their insistence on reliving biblical Christianity means that they are not as discontinuous as the Charismatic churches may want the world to believe. In a recent study of the CMs, Paul Gifford points out that more than 90% of the sermons in the new churches centre on the Old Testament.[10] Baëta had much earlier made a similar observation of the Spiritual churches, noting that in the Spiritual churches, where reversions to African traditional practices had taken place, they were attributed to 'the authority of the Old Testament rather than the fact that the customs were African.'[11] The contribution of Ghana's Spiritual churches to African Christianity lies not only in the inculturation processes they initiated, but also in the strong emphasis that a number of them placed on the moral demands of the faith including their obstinate stance against the consumption of alcohol and irresponsible parenthood. Some of the changes that have occurred in Ghanaian Christianity in particular since the publication of *Prophetism in Ghana* are also noteworthy because they enable us appreciate the sharpness of Baëta's prophetic insight which is articulated in the findings of his study.

First, under pressure from the forceful impact of the AICs, the historic mission churches, from the late 1960s, started incorporating elements like handclapping, dancing, locally-composed Christian choruses, prayer vigils, and healing into their otherwise ordered and formalized worship services and liturgical structures. Historic mission churches also started tolerating charismatic renewal movements within their own churches in an attempt to respond to the challenge of the presence of the AICs and to stem the steady drift of their members to the new African churches as places 'to feel at home.' The Presbyterian Church of Ghana in 1965 and the Methodist Church, Ghana in 1969 actually discussed the challenges of the presence of the Spiritual churches to their own ministries and established committees to study them and to evaluate for emulation what benefits they could derive from the popular worship services and interventionist theologies of the independent churches they previously despised. The changes have come full circle with the tolerance of renewal movements within historic mission denominations, the rise of new Charismatic churches, and the transformation of some AICs into CMs as a way of ensuring their own survival in the midst of modernity and change. The benefits of the renewal initiated by the Spiritual churches have thus been mutual.

Second, except for South Africa's Zionist churches, the AICs have been on the decline since the 1970s. At a time when several scholars and theologians were considering whether the AICs were the future of African Christianity, Baëta had already noticed the 'approaching fatigue' in these churches and virtually predicted their demise. That prediction has also come to pass as evidenced by two Ghana Evangelism Committee surveys conducted in 1986 and 1991. Within the five-year period of the surveys, attendance at the services of both the Apostles Revelation Society and the Musama Disco Christo Church had declined by 17%. Attendance at the Sacred Order of the Cherubim and Seraphim declined by 24%, in the African Faith Tabernacle by 23%, and the Church of the Twelve Apostles by 22%. The reasons for the dwindling fortunes of the Spiritual churches include the deaths and incapacitation of their charismatic prophetic leaders around whose personalities and gifts the churches revolved, the lack of ecclesial structures like youth and children's ministries that would have ensured the natural supply of members, and the focus on healing and prophecy at the expense of Christian discipleship through serious evangelism, expository preaching and theological education. Reference has already been made to the metamorphosis into CMs in an attempt to adopt a more modern outlook. The problem-solving orientation of the ministries of the Spiritual churches meant that they attracted large numbers of floating members who kept moving from prophet to prophet in search of solutions to their problems. A number of Spiritual churches have also split up for reasons ranging from lack of accountability to succession-related acrimonious conflicts at the deaths of the founders of these churches. For instance, the African Faith Tabernacle popularly called 'Nkansah' after its leader Prophet James Kwame Nkansah was one of the churches studied by Baëta. This church has, since the death of the prophet in 1987, experienced succession problems that have led to splits into, at least, five factions.[12]

Third, since the publication of *Prophetism in Ghana*, the ministry of the prophet as a key religious functionary has re-emerged within modern forms of indigenous Pentecostalism represented by the new Charismatic churches. Gifford discusses the nature and ministry of the new prophets in his book, *Ghana's New Christianity*.[13] This new manifestation of prophetism within modern Ghanaian Christianity is remarkable when considered in the light of the predictions made by Baëta more than three decades ago. His thoughts on the matter are worth quoting in full:

> *[Prophetism] appears to me to be a perennial phenomenon of African life, and the basic operative element in it seems to be personal in character. Whether in relation to or independently of events or developments in society, the individual endowed with a striking personality and the ability to impose his own will on others, believing himself, and believed by others to be a special agent of some supernatural being or force, will emerge from time to time and secure a following. Powers traditionally credited to such persons, of healing, revealing hidden things, predicting the future, cursing and blessing effectually, etc., will be attributed to him whether he claims them or not. Some will make a more successful showing than others. Such things as the above-mentioned endowment, inward illumination, a sense of divine vocation, spontaneous enthusiasm... are facts of life and have their effects in African society.*[14]

That *Prophetism in Ghana* has remained relevant in the midst of the changes discussed is a result of the very prophetic insights that Baëta brought to his study. He wrote with clairvoyance, guided by a very unique ability to look at the Spiritual churches and predict what the nature, impact, and future trend of the development of these movements were likely to be.

The Spiritual churches may be declining numerically as I have noted earlier, but their diminishing physical presence has not erased their unique contribution to African theology. In fact, their qualitative impact on Ghanaian Christianity continues through an enduring religious and theological heritage. This heritage is evident through the initiation of an effective inculturation process, the normalization of charismatic experiences in Christian expression and worship, a more practical view of salvation, the use of oral theology, and an innovative gender ideology in which, for the first time, women became founders and leaders of Christian churches in Africa. Perhaps the greatest contribution of the Spiritual churches to Christianity in Ghana is that they bridged the gap that formerly existed between primal spirituality and Christianity. In contrast to Western Christian theologies that seem on the whole to be a system of ideas, primal religions, according to Ghanaian theologian Kwame Bediako, are generally conceived 'as a system of power and of living religiously as being in touch with the source and channels of power in the universe.'[15] In primal religiosity, finite human beings stand in need of the powers and blessings of benevolent transcendent powers, and draw on such sources for protection from evil forces through appropriate covenant relationships with such transcendent benevolent helpers.

The Spiritual churches became popular in African countries like Ghana because they affirmed the reality of God and other supernatural entities. Destructive and malevolent powers seeking to destroy people and angels representing the Christian equivalent of transcendent benevolent powers both featured prominently in the worldview of the Spiritual churches. That into the twenty-first century the theology that seems to have become characteristic of the African church is that which takes seriously the pneumatic experiences of the Bible in general and the New Testament in particular, underscores the veracity of many of Baëta's findings. The renewal occurring within Ghanaian Christianity has been such that even those churches that stand in historic continuity with Western missions and, and which have inherited their rationalistic, systematic, and creedal forms of Christianity as I have noted, have been forced to take charismatic renewal seriously. The process has involved a rethinking of traditional church pneumatologies including a practical articulation of a response to the reality of evil, a non-negotiable element in the religious consciousness of all Christians who are alive to the world of the Bible. In this way Africa, through the ingenuity of the African independent church movement and typified by the Spiritual churches, has emerged as the new centre of theological creativity, 'a laboratory' as Bediako calls it, where 'Christian answers to African questions are hammered out.'[16] We owe our understanding of African-initiated Christianity to scholars like Baëta, who drew attention to the Spiritual churches, and affirmed them as truly indigenous Christian movements whose innovative Christianity had much to teach about what it meant to be African and Christian at the same time without undermining any of these twin identities.

The world has certainly not heard the final word on independent indigenous Christianity in Africa. Within the last decade alone, several publications have emerged on various aspects of Christian religious innovation on the continent and there is reason to believe that there are several more on the way. Wherever the story of religious innovation in Africa is told, Baëta's contribution will continue to be an important part of the historical analysis. So we will continue to encounter him from his place as part of the 'cloud of witnesses' urging on modern scholars in the perennial quest for what lies embedded in indigenous African Christianity that God wants preserved during this period when the centre of gravity of the Christian faith has so decidedly - to use the words of Barrett, Walls and Bediako - shifted from the northern to the southern continents.

J. Kwabena Asamoah-Gyadu, PhD
Trinity Theological Seminary, Legon, Ghana.
September 2004.

NOTES

[1] Harold W. Turner, Review of *Prophetism in Ghana*, in *International Review of Mission*, 53 (1964), 94.
[2] The African Theological Fellowship (ATF) is a fraternity of African scholars founded by Professor Kwame Bediako of the Akrofi-Christaller Centre for Mission Research and Applied Theology, in the mid 1980s. ATF academic consultations centre on developments within African Christianities and theologies and they take place at various locations on the continent. Prof. Kwame Bediako is the General Secretary and the present author of this foreword is the coordinator for the West Africa sub-region.
[3] J. Kwabena Asamoah-Gyadu, *African Charismatics: A Study of some Current Developments within Independent Indigenous Pentecostalism in Ghana* (Leiden: E.J. Brill, 2004).
[4] Adrian Hastings, 'Christianity in Africa', in Ursula King (ed.), *Turning Points in Religious Studies: Essays in Honor of Geoffrey Parrinder* (Edinburgh: T&T Clarke, 1990), 204.
[5] C.G. Baëta, 'Christianity and Healing', *Orita*, vol. 1 (1967), 53.
[6] Baëta, *Prophetism in Ghana: A Study of some Spiritual Churches* (London: SCM, 1962), 135.
[7] Baëta, *Prophetism in Ghana*, 135.
[8] Kalu, Ogbu U. 'The Third Response: Pentecostalism and the Reconstruction of Christian Experience in Africa', *Journal of African Christian Thought*, vol. 1, 2 (1998), 3-16.
[9] Andrew F. Walls, *The Missionary Movement in Christian History: Studies in the Transmission of Faith* (Maryknoll, NY: Orbis, 1996), 93.
[10] Paul Gifford, *Ghana's New Christianity: Pentecostalism in a Globalizing African Economy* (Bloomington and Indianapolis: Indiana University Press, 2004), 71-82.

[11] Baëta, *Prophetism in Ghana*, 128.
[12] Asamoah-Gyadu, *African Charismatics*, chapter 3.
[13] Paul Gifford, *Ghana's New Christianity*, 89-112, 186.
[14] Baëta, *Prophetism in Ghana*, 6-7.
[15] Kwame Bediako, *Christianity in Africa: The Renewal of a Non-Western Religion* (Edinburgh: Edinburgh University Press; Maryknoll, NY: Orbis Books, 1995), 106.
[16] Kwame Bediako, interviewed by Kim A. Lawton, 'Faith without Borders: How the Developing World is Changing the Face of Christianity,' *Christianity Today* (May 19, 1997), 44.

PREFACE

THE various Christian sectarian groups outside their own folds have been an object of great concern to the old and well-established churches in Ghana for years. The latter's view of the former is on the whole negative, being that they constitute a grave menace to the normal development of a healthy type of Christianity in the country. But there is little or no precise knowledge of them. Apart from two or three rather slight magazine articles written by newspaper reporters, there is nothing about them in print.[1]

Who are they? What are their origins, beliefs and practices? What promises and hopes do they hold out? Who go to them and what happens when they do? How are they organized, controlled, nurtured, maintained? In how far are they viable and serious rivals of, and alternatives to, the older churches? In short, just what is there to know about them?

The primary aim of this study was to find and make available in somewhat adequate detail, information which might afford answers to the questions posed. It seemed worthwhile doing this even if the results proved to be covered, in broad general terms, by the descriptions already available of similar groups in other lands. The details, bound to be different, might well yield some new points of interest. This in fact turned out to be the case.

In any event if, as may be presumed, the older churches recognize a duty to assist these bodies to enter fully into the Church Universal, and become adequate expressions of Christian faith and life, then it would appear that the least they can do for a start is to take knowledge of them.

Despite their confusingly similar cultic behaviour, the groups in question divide easily into those which were established and are still managed by foreign agencies (British and American) and those which have come into being as the result of indigenous African prophetism. There is also a marginal group of bodies with names of foreign sects but no significant relation to them. They were started either by local people who had read or otherwise learnt of these societies abroad, and wanted to establish branches in Ghana, or by foreign agents sent here to establish them.

The groups introduced from foreign countries appear to be more or less exact transplantations of their parent organizations. Since these are already covered by a considerable literature, it seemed desirable to restrict the scope of the present study to the groups of local origin.

PREFACE

This leaves out such important groups as the Apostolic Church of Ghana and its splinter-body the Ghana Apostolic Church, neither does it take account of the interesting establishment known as 'The Lord is there Temple' (formerly 'The Divine Healer's Temple') which, with its powerful loudspeakers, is such a notable feature of night-life at Korlegonno, Accra, and which, at daybreak every Sunday, admits scores of converts into the Apostolic connection by mass baptisms in the sea.

A note on the manner of gathering and presenting this material may be of interest. As in Tacitus' day new religious movements from all over the Roman Empire congregated in the metropolis, so today such movements in Ghana converge on Accra. All the bodies with which we are concerned are represented in the capital. That was extremely convenient for me when I first started on my investigations because, living only eight miles out at Legon, I could easily go down and take a first look at each of them. For a number of months I drove into Accra two or three evenings each week to visit the various groups at their meetings.

When I joined the worshippers, I always took care to slip in as unobtrusively as possible; but often I stood outside with the crowd of curious onlookers always present to watch the proceedings. Usually my presence was completely ignored, but sometimes I had the feeling that the elaborate apology for, or justification of, what was being done, or the severe strictures upon the 'historical churches' made by the speakers, were being intended particularly for my benefit, an opinion confirmed by the fact that, at the specially pungent remarks several members of the congregation would turn around to look at me, and then whisper to their neighbour! I believe I always managed to maintain a glacial calm. However, when I met leaders in personal interviews, there was never once any unpleasantness or inveighing against anybody or anything, only the greatest friendliness and willingness to co-operate.

In the circumstances, no method of study was open to me except visiting, observing and questioning. I visited several times the headquarters of all the organizations here discussed, and many of their outstations as well. I met and conversed at length with the acknowledged head of each one of all the major groups; I also had separate and long sessions with their leading personalities sitting together with the acknowledged head. I checked information received at headquarters by questioning outstation representatives, and vice versa. I saw practically all the ceremonies and activities usually performed, and read everything the groups had published which was still available. I spoke with many people who had experience of the group: believers and disbelievers in all degrees, and the indifferent. My assistants went to live for a few days at a time in areas of greatest influence of the various groups, where my own presence would doubtless have attracted undue notice; they had for their guidance a carefully prepared and very fully discussed questionnaire. Apart from securing answers to the questions

PREFACE

listed they were to engage casually in conversation with all and sundry about the activities of the groups and to try to discover what people thought of them. I afterwards checked upon whatever information turned up which was new to me excepting, of course, the opinions reported from conversations.

I have discussed the major groups in chronological order of their emergence, and each one in two or three sections, my aim being, as far as possible, to keep reported information, observed fact, and opinion, distinctly separate. Where the group concerned has a substantial story of its own to tell, I have put that into the first section. Then follows a section describing factually my observations, and giving all the information of general interest that I was able to obtain about the group. Where the group does not have a substantial story this section, together with some history, of course becomes the first. The last section on each group consists of my comments on points which I consider to be worthy of note. There is one chapter, of summary accounts only, of groups on the fringes of my sphere of investigation; in this chapter the plan just outlined is not followed. Finally, in the concluding chapter of the whole study, I have sought to sum up my impressions in a general way, attempting a characterization and an interpretation of the entire phenomenon of Ghanaian prophetism, and showing in which ways it stands out, both from similar movements elsewhere and from orthodox Christianity.

Without the courteous co-operation of the leaders of the various churches which I have studied, my work would have been very much more difficult, perhaps even impossible. They all received me with the greatest friendliness and gave me not only hospitality but also many, many hours of their valuable time. Sometimes considerable expense must have been incurred in calling the meetings of leading personalities for my benefit, as some members travelled from distant places to attend. Our discussions were frank and hearty, and we usually ended up with exchanges of views on points of doctrines or policy, in the manner of those engaged in a common search. I greatly enjoyed these meetings. I usually began by emphasizing that I was not coming as a representative of the Christian Council, and above all that I did not want any argument; the sole object of my visit was to collect information, in order that our students at the University might learn the true facts of the religious situation in the country. I illustrated by mentioning various projects undertaken by other University Departments to collect local materials in their own fields. This point was always very well received.

Several other friends gave me most valuable assistance in diverse ways. My former colleagues at the University College of Ghana, Dr. G. Jahoda and the late Dr. David Tait, with great experience in these matters, helped me to define the area of my investigations. The College gave me a generous grant which, apart from making possible my extensive travels within the country, enabled me to employ (one at a time and for short periods only) the late Mr. B. K. Djantor and Mr. M. E. Kofi Biako as research assistants.

PREFACE

Dr. R. Pierce Beaver, of the Federated Theological Faculty of the University of Chicago, USA, to whom, in a conversation during a walk at Davos, Switzerland, I mentioned what I was trying to do, sent me, on his return home, ten volumes of the most outstanding works on the smaller sects in his own country. These highly informative books were a source of great enlightenment for me at many points.

My colleagues and friends Professor K.A. Busia, Professor N. Q. King and Dr. S. G. Williamson helped me with criticisms, suggestions, and encouragement, and by drawing my attention to any groups that they heard of which seemed to come within my area of study, and Dr. Hans Debrunner very kindly acquainted me with various relevant books. From the outset I had planned to spend the first three years of my study mainly on the fieldwork, reserving the fourth year for writing. It was providential that for this final year of my preparation I should have been invited by President H.P. Van Dusen of Union Theological Seminary, New York City, to come to this great institution as the year's Henry W. Luce visiting Professor of World Christianity. This withdrawal from my many involvements at home, with a diminished teaching commitment, enabled me to sort out my field notes and write them up more conveniently than would doubtless have been the case if I had remained in Ghana. I have been particularly privileged at Union Seminary to have at my disposal the world-famous Missionary Research Library which contains not only the larger works relevant to my purpose, but also all sorts of smaller publications, periodicals, monographs, unpublished typescripts, etc., of the greatest interest for my work. Dr. Frank W. Price, the Director of this Library, and his staff, were most co-operative and kind.

Finally I would mention my friend Professor M. Searle Bates, of Union Seminary, and Professor M. Guthrie, of the London University School of Oriental and African Studies, from whom I received expert guidance. For all this help so generously given my gratitude is unbounded.

The substance of the little volume now presented was approved as a thesis for the Doctor of Philosophy degree in the Divinity Faculty of the University of London. The original text has been adjusted and abridged mainly from the point of view of avoiding offence. If, however, this book should still contain anything painful to any persons I hereby offer apology and assure them that such an effect was never intended.

C.G.B.

NOTES

[1] On the Church of the Twelve Apostles in *The African Challenge* for April 1957, and on the Apostolic Revelation Society in *African World* for July 1957. The latter article is the basis of C. P. Groves, *The Planting of Christianity in Africa*, vol. IV, p.353f.

CHAPTER ONE

Introduction

Definitions

NOBODY interested in the actual practice of religion in Ghana today can fail to take notice of the large numbers of people who attach themselves to the groups generally known as 'separatist churches.' In his book Religion in an African City, Dr. G. Parrinder describes separatist church as follows: 'These are sects which have split away from, or sprung up in relative independence of, the older mission churches' (page 107).

This definition would cover all the groups with which we are here concerned. In Ghana, however, the leaders of these bodies, on the whole, appear to dislike the designation of 'separatist churches' and much prefer to be known as 'spiritual' churches. What is meant is doubtless more correctly described as 'spiritist' than as 'spiritual,' but common usage has adopted the latter adjective. In this context the word 'spiritual' has a very special connotation which must be explained. It is intended to signify that, in their worship, the groups concerned engage in various activities which (by their own assertion) are either meant to invoke the Holy Spirit of God, or are to be interpreted as signs of his descent upon the worshippers. Under 'What we believe and teach,' for example, the Ghana Apostolic Church almanac for the year 1958 lists as point No. 5: '*The baptism of the Holy Ghost for believers, with signs following.*'

These activities and 'signs' include rhythmic swaying of the body, usually with stamping, to repetitious music (both vocal and instrumental, particularly percussion), hand-clappings, ejaculations, poignant cries and prayers, dancing, leaping, and various motor reactions expressive of intense religious emotion; prophesyings, 'speaking with tongues,' falling into trances, relating dreams and visions, and 'witnessing,' i.e. recounting publicly one's own experience of miraculous redemption.

The application of the term 'spiritual churches' is popularly extended to embrace also bodies whose interests are by no means 'spiritual' in the sense defined, notably 'Jehovah's Witnesses.' This is partly because outsiders, ignorant of the differences between the various unorthodox bodies, tend to lump them all together; partly also it is due to a common supposition that 'spiritual churches' is merely a courtesy term which is preferred to 'sects' because the people concerned regard the latter word as having a disparaging flavour.[1] However, this distinction need not concern us further, as our present interest is limited to groups which are all (though in various degrees) 'spiritual churches' in the sense indicated.[2]

The inclusive term in use in Ghana for the bodies which Dr. Parrinder has called 'the older mission churches' is 'the historical churches.' I propose to retain it for this study.

Some Opinions of the Sects

Several evaluations have been made of the significance of what has been called 'the whole painful problem posed by the existence and rapid growth of the "Separatist" churches.' Dr. B. N. G. Sundkler states that his interest in undertaking his own study had been 'based on the assumption that, in these churches, one would be able to see what the African Christian, when left to himself, regarded as important and relevant in Christian faith and in the Christian church. By such a study I hoped to be able to discern tendencies that could be utilized in the practical task of building Christ's Church in Africa.'[3]

In a review of Dr. G. Parrinder's book Religion in an African City, the late Dr. E. W. Smith makes more or less the same point regarding 'these dissident societies' and continues as follows: 'Their success is due in no small measure to their adoption of less formal, more lively, forms of worship with the use of native music and instruments–They approach nearer the African ethos whereas the churches of European and dull.'[4]

In an article on 'The Church's Duty to Separatist Religious Sects'[5] the Rev. E. A. Maycock also writes: '... But new sects have also arisen sometimes because of a lack of sympathetic understanding of local problems on the part of the authorities of the parent church itself... it is wise to enquire sometimes...whether there is anything which the parent churches can learn from them.'

Dr. J. W. C. Dougall's comprehensive and excellent review of the whole subject[6] contains many passages which are highly relevant in the present connection. I adduce only his introductory paragraph: 'The study of African separatist churches has many attractions, both theoretical and practical. These curious movements possess features which are of interest to the student of primitive religion. They reveal the possibilities and the risks of revival movements under genuine African leadership and they are of great significance for the guidance of the younger churches when they seek to become truly indigenous in character and method. Moreover, the study of the way in which these movements begin and develop is of some help in the study of the relation of Christianity to culture, both Western and African, and throws up a number of clues to the whole problem of adaptation and syncretism in the world mission of the Church.'

It may not be out of place to consider and comment upon these opinions and expectations in the light of the facts of the Ghana situation. This has been woven into the concluding chapter.

Background to the Subject

In the first place, a clear distinction should be made between prophetism and messianism. No doubt much prophetism is messianic: the stimulus to the prophet's vocation is often provided by intolerable social, political, or religious conditions, or a combination of these; by any threats to the continuing existence of the prophet's society or its culture, through the seemingly irresistible encroachments of a stronger alien group or culture. The messianic message, born of such a threat, usually proclaims the imminent arrival to the menaced community of supernatural help, either in the form of a personal deliverer who would triumph over all their foes, or in that of some blow of catastrophic misfortune and destruction to be dealt to the invading forces by supernatural means. As such situations of dire foreboding, helplessness and desperation have abounded for African societies since the intrusion of foreign peoples, there have been many messianic movements on the continent.

For this reason the whole phenomenon of prophetism and separatist churches has been linked very closely with the conflict between European rulers and their subject peoples. In practically all accounts of them, from the earliest moments in Central and Southern Africa to contemporary ones among the Ba-kongo in the Belgian Congo and French Equatorial Africa (whose frustrations and inward agonies are so poignantly described by G. Balandier), their significance in this context has been almost unanimously noted and stressed.[7] In fact, prophets and their dissident churches seem now to be generally regarded as a 'standard element in Africa 'nationalism,' i.e. the resistance to, or rejection of, European control.[8] For Southern Africa Dr. Sundkler has ascribed their rise to the complete absence of any other opportunities open to the Negro citizens for political or even social self-expression. Comparable movements in other continents, such as the Cargo cults of Melanesia and the Indian Shaker cults of North America have likewise been shown to be products of the reaction against the impingement of Caucasian imperialism.

But that is not all of prophetism. Prophetism arises from the dream or vision of a prophet, and this is not necessarily, or in fact always, related to prevailing external conditions. It may be (and often is) entirely a matter of personal inward, usually religions, experience or development. For instance, clearly the major pre-occupation of Mr. Doh, leader of the Etodome group (he does not wish to be called a 'prophet'), is to find the means whereby men may hold converse with God on their day-to-day concerns. Again, the following excerpt from the welcome address given by the head of the Musama Disco Christo Church to his people assembled for the 1957 celebration of that Church's annual great festival, illustrates the prevalence in many cases of interests which cannot be otherwise described but as religious:

> *You all who are present, I bring you to the full understanding that the PEACEFUL YEAR Anniversary is of more spiritual meaning than we can explain. It has no reference to political or economical Peace. It is an Anniversary for the Army of the Cross of Christ (Musama Disco Christo) to assemble and to account for the goodness of God upon His children, the victory of the Christians and the Grace that still sustains THE Hope of the followers of 'That-Which-Is-Good.' It is a gathering to strengthen our faith and to prove to ourselves that Christ is NOT ONLY a God of Salvation of the Soul BUT ALSO a Father that is prepared to meet all our needs (Matthew 6: 11, 13; Psalm 91:11,15).*

In Ghana the nearest thing to a messianic-prophetic movement of which I have any knowledge is the Bensu sect, which clashed with Government Police at Agona-Swedru in November of 1932. In the ensuing scuffle each side lost one man by death, with several others injured. The members of this sect, under their leader, a certain Prophet Appiah, had declared their intention of marching to Accra (a distance of over 40 miles) to set free all the prisoners held in Ussher Fort Prison; the police insisted on their disbanding. But even this is not a good example because, as far as I was able to ascertain, the Bensu-ites were animated, not so much by opposition to British rule as by obedience to what they understood to be a scriptural injunction to them, namely to set all captives free.[9]

It must be borne in mind that the religious is, at least, as deep a human interest as any other. The enterprise in which the present sects of Ghana appear to be engaged, namely an all-out effort to probe the reality of spiritual things, is a genuine and fully intelligible human quest in its own right.

In the summary of her book Propheten in Afrika (p. 401) Katesa Schlosser states: 'Apart from purely personal ambition, the reasons for the appearance of prophets are predominantly of an economic and political nature, exclusively religious only in the rarest cases.' Human motivation would seem to be, at any time, complex and mixed, rather than 'purely' or 'exclusively' one thing or another. If the prophets whose preponderant interest was religious appear to have been few, it must be remembered that those who have assembled the data at present available have been, for the most part, persons primarily interested in, and on the lookout for, any happenings which might have political import. Personalities and groups in whose activities no such significance is discernible would tend to be ignored, or only smiled at indulgently.

In the book just mentioned, for example, only three prophets are recorded for Ghana, namely Opong, Chei and Danso. But most People in the country will have encountered several others of these remarkable figures roaming the countryside, making their dramatic appearance and delivering their messages at the road junctions and marketplaces, and in the villages. Usually their dress is a long, flowing robe of some cheap material, with a cross or some other symbol sewn on to it; also they would usually wear a beard and carry a staff. The account of the Musama Disco Christo Church in this story refers to two such 'minor' prophets, Nyankson and Dankwa. The story of the first is told, in part, in that account; the following gathered by the second has dwindled to such insignificance that it was not considered worthwhile to include it in this survey, through the sensational incident that its only known remaining pastor was shot dead by one of his own parishioners. It will now probably become quite extinct. From the 1920's to the 1930's there flourished a considerable prophetic movement called Abibipim (African Universal Church) which has now faded out, leaving hardly a trace, and doubtless there have been smaller ones that have suffered the same fate. The conclusion must be that half the story has not been told, and such a generalization as the one at present under discussion must be received with caution.

The rise of ever-new cults to meet the prevailing spiritual and emotional needs of the people is a well-established feature of African life, some periods throwing up more prolific outcrops than others. The 'spiritual churches' may be seen as standing in this tradition. They provide a new recourse particularly for the mentally not-so-tough in the various ills that afflict them as they try to adjust to the rapidly changing conditions and demands of modern economic and social life. However, there is no confusion between physician and patient. In my opinion it would be very wide of the mark indeed to suppose that the people forming the core of these churches are persons suffering any psychological malaise, or extraordinary emotional strains and stresses. Rather they appear to be perfectly normal, even 'relaxed' men and women, taking the new developments in their stride, coping with their ordinary human problems as best they know how, likewise taking in hand, with a quite practical outlook and high degree of self-confidence, what they consider to be their job, namely healing as they understand it.

It appears to me that in recent studies of new cults and other movements of a religious nature among African peoples, the presumed background element of psychological upheaval, tensions and conflicts, anxieties, etc., due to 'acculturation, technology and the Western impact' has tended to be rather overdrawn. Here is a typical judgment in this connection: '...the situation in modern Ashanti is such that individuals are bound to feel, almost continually, some form of anxiety – in economic life, in kinship relations, in politics...Any student of society would expect to find, in such a situation, a considerable recourse to the supernatural for reassurance and the establishment of confidence and for the explanation of failures and unpredictable occurrences.[10] Whether there is more anxiety in Ghana now than at any time previously, or than in most other countries of the world at present, must probably remain a matter of opinion. After all, people have seen some very rough times here, e.g. the slaving era, and the 'Western impact' has been with us already for the best part of half a millennium, though admittedly in recent years its actual impingement has gathered tremendous momentum.

However, prophetism appears to me to be a perennial phenomenon of African life, and the basic operative element in it seems to be personal in character. Whether in relation to or independently of events or developments in society, the individual endowed with a striking personality and the ability to impose his own will on others, believing himself, and believed by others to be a special agent of some supernatural being or force, will emerge from time to time and secure a following. Powers traditionally credited to such persons, of healing, of revealing hidden things, predicting the future, cursing and blessing effectually, etc., will be attributed to him whether he claims them or not. Some will make a more successful showing than others. Such things as the above-mentioned endowment, inward

INTRODUCTION 7

illumination, a sense of divine vocation, spontaneous enthusiasm (in the original sense of being in God, experiencing ardent religious zeal) are facts of life and have their effects in African society.

It is the special merit of Katesa Schlosser's book already referred to, that it illustrates this point by taking its 'prophets' from all the historical periods at all relevantly documented, as well as from the spheres of all the religions professed in Africa.

NOTES
1. Where the word 'sects' appears in this study it has no such pejorative implication.
2. A very useful classification of the different types of sects is carried out in Elmer T. Clark, The Small Sects in America (Abingdon-Cokesbury). See particularly the Index and Chapter 1.
3. B. M. G. Sundkler, Bantu Prophets in South Africa, p. 17f.
4. Africa, vol. xxiv, 1, p. 70.
5. In The Daystar (now defunct) for April 1955, p. 6f.
6. In an article in the International Review of Missions for July, 1956.
7. George Shepperson, 'The Politics of African Church Separatist Movements, in British Central Africa 1892-1916', in Africa, vol. xxiv, 3, p. 233f. And most of the other literature given in the Bibliography; G. Balandier, Afrique Ambigue (Plon). The following remark is interesting as representing a point of view different from the usual one. (My own translation) 'In general, the black churches do not have any programmes hostile to white people; only, since they often arise as a results of unpleasant incidents and quarrels with white pastors, they naturally become centres for malcontents.' R. P. Alexandre Brou, S.J, 'Le Prophetisme dans les eglises protestantes indigenes d' Afrique', Revue d' Histoire des Missions, VIIIe annee, 1, p. 73.
8. In an excellent chapter entitled 'Prophets and Priests', these movements are listed as the third major factor in Nationalism in Colonial Africa, in a book of this title by Thomas Hodgkin (Frederick Muller, London). This book has a most helpful bibliography on this and other aspects of African affairs.
9. This affair was a source of great embarrassment for the Musama Disco Christo Church. Since its leader was also called Prophet Appiah, both Government and the general public confused the two, and leading members of this Church at various stations were promptly arrested. The misunderstanding was soon cleared, of course, and this body now cherishes a letter to them from the Provincial Commissioner's representative to the effect that so long as they maintained the peace and made earnest endeavours to promote the welfare of their members, they need not fear any opposition from the Government.
10. Barbara E. Ward, 'Some Observations on Religious Cults in Ashanti', in Africa vol. xxvi pp. 47-61.

CHAPTER TWO

The Church of the Twelve Apostles

THIS group, popularly referred to in the Western Province of Ghana as Nackabah, is practically unknown elsewhere, although its leaders claim members 'scattered all over Ghana.' Outside observers also have the impression that their numbers are increasing rapidly, but no definite figures are available. As a religious body they are interesting, not only for their present activities, but also because they constitute a continuing result of a visit paid to the Apollonia and Axim districts of the then Gold Coast by the well-known Grebo (Kru) prophet William Wade Harris, as far back as the year 1914. The group therefore claims to be the "first of the 'spiritual churches' in Ghana." Their official name derives from the practice of Harris to appoint '...twelve Apostles in each village to look after the needs of the flock.'[1] But although the name is preserved, the practice itself has been discontinued, or altered beyond recognition.[2]

Some History

Among the converts made and baptized by Harris on his visit were a woman by the name of Grace Tani, a native of Ankobra Mouth, and John Nackabah of Essuawua near Enchi. Nackabah in turn baptized John Hackman, an illiterate pagan. All three persons had gifts of 'prophecy' and spiritual healing, and together they founded the Church of the Twelve Apostles in Ghana. Although Grace Tani was really the moving spirit, Nackabah was more prominently in the public eye, which resulted in people coming to call the group by his name. The present leaders, though not expressing any resentment of this name, seem to look upon it as a misnomer, and would regularly correct it to 'Twelve Apostles' when it is mentioned.

After the deaths of Grace Tani and Nackabah, leadership passed on to John Hackman, who made his seat at Kadjabir on the way to Mpoho, 12 miles from Sekondi. This place came to be regarded as the headquarters of the whole connection. All the most important conferences have been held there and, up to recently, it was there that the connection had its only considerable chapel building. This is a whitewashed rectangular structure in swish and corrugated iron sheets, measuring some 55 by 25 feet; the shape of the windows and the interior arrangement follow the general pattern common for Methodist chapels in Ghana.

Until his death on 2nd June 1957, John Hackman was the undisputed head of the 'Twelve Apostles,' having lived in close fellowship with Grace Tani and Nackabah, who hold the pre-eminent place in the minds of the members not only as the founders and earliest leaders, but also as the ones most highly endowed with 'spirit.' Nackabah himself made Hackman 'Bishop' shortly before he died. Bishop Hackman in turn transferred his powers to his nephew, Samuel Kofi Ansah, who, at the time of the former's death, was only a minor prophet stationed at the small village of Aboadi. In true African tradition of the appointment of leaders, however, he also had to be elected by the people over whom he was to have authority.

As the aged Hackman's impaired health showed no signs of improvement, the senior prophets of the four districts were summoned to Kadjabir for the purpose of electing his successor. Hackman indicated his choice. There was wake-keeping that day (a Thursday) with prayers and singing throughout the night until dawn, an exercise that was repeated the following day. On Saturday, Ansah was unanimously elected, and Hackman blessed him ceremoniously in the presence of the Supreme Church Committee, the assembled prophets, and many others who had, in the meantime, foregathered at Kadjabir. The ceremony was concluded with the presentation to the new Bishop, by the senior prophets, of his staff of office and authority. This is a plain wooden staff surmounted by a simple cross; it is about the same length as a bishop's crook but is not hooked at the top. Hackman died soon afterwards.

Bishop Ansah, a mild man and utterly illiterate, apparently did not prove to be of sufficient stature to command respect and exercise full authority. During his term of office, some of the district senior prophets arrogated to themselves the title of bishop and conducted their affairs with scant, if any, reference to Kadjabir. Apart from insubordination, nepotism is reported to have been rife; people, when reprimanded, pointing out that after all the Bishop was himself Hackman's nephew.[3]

Bishop Ansah died in June 1958 without having made any firm arrangements for a successor.

Church Organization, Finance, and Displine

The Twelve Apostles Church now counts four districts with head-stations as follows:

1. Ahanta district, head-station Kadjabir, with 33 sub-stations; 2. Fanti district, head-station Kromantyne near Saltpond, with 65 sub-stations; 3. Nzima district, head-station Ankobra mouth; and 4. Gwira-Wassaw district, head-station Essuawua. For some time the leaders of the two last-named districts have refused to go to Kadjabir for meetings or to communicate any information regarding themselves, but they are known to be continuing to function as actively as ever. Each district is now practically independent, though they all continue in the same habits and practices as before. Within each district, a seven-man committee meets once every three months to regulate the affairs of the district, but since Hackman's death only the Fanti and Ahanta districts have been able to hold joint meetings. Even these have been extremely difficult to lead, owing to the indiscipline of many of the prophets, each claiming inspiration of the 'spirit' to do as he thinks fit. There is now no central organization for, or pooling of, the finances of the connection, not even at the district level. Each prophet or healer simply keeps the thanksgiving offerings of his patients for himself. Apart from collections taken at the church services, members pay a monthly levy of sixpence (6d) per adult, and a harvest celebration is held once a year.

Infraction of Church regulations is punished with suspension for up to three months, depending upon the seriousness of the offence. Sometimes it is insisted that the offender ask for forgiveness publicly and offer a packet of candles before readmission to full membership is conceded. In such cases a special prayer session is held on behalf of the person concerned.

Educational Standards and Training

The educational standards in the Twelve Apostles Church are the lowest of any non-pagan religious body in Ghana. Most of the prophets and healers are completely illiterate: of 34 prophets in the Ahanta district, only five are literate in Fanti; apart from the leader of the Sekondi-Ketan group, none can read English, and no local leader in the whole sect has attained the educational standard of the elementary school leaving certificate. The Fanti branch recently declared that, before consecration to the office of prophet, candidates would in future be required to be literate, at least in their own native tongue, which is usually Fanti. This branch is now availing itself of the facilities for adult literacy offered by the Government Department of Social Welfare, to have its 15 trainees instructed in reading and writing Fanti. This general illiteracy of its leaders is responsible for the fact that no records of any kind have been kept of this sect. The only official documents in print at present are the 'Charter'[4] and the membership card. A catechism, hymnbook and service-book, all in Fanti, are said to be in preparation.⁵

All training proceeds through 'learning by doing.' Members who show both aptitude and a desire for the 'prophetic' calling must go and live at some 'Garden' and practice what they observe. One leader stated that, while the external acts and ceremonies are quickly learnt, long exercise is necessary to enable trainees to offer effective prayers and to keep the fast rigidly.

Leading Personalities

The two most outstanding men of this connection at present, and at the same time those with the liveliest local groups, are the leaders of Sekondi-Ketan and Kromantyne. The first, Mr. Henry Gladstone Nerbah Nathan, was born in 1886 of very staunch and religiously fervent Methodist parents, natives of Dixcove. He himself was baptized in the Methodist Church and attended the Methodist local school of his hometown. In 1902 he left home to join his uncle, a timber contractor living at Grand Bassam in the French Ivory Coast, for work. When Prophet Harris was at the height of his preaching career, Nathan came under the spell of his influence. He was one of the scores of thousands who were converted and baptized (in his case it was re-baptism) by Harris without receiving any Christian instruction. That happened in 1914. During World War I, Nathan was recruited in the Ivory Coast as a French colonial soldier, and served both in France and with the French occupation troops in Germany. He returned to his homeland of Ghana in 1925, and was employed by the Government Department of Agriculture as an assistant inspector of plants and produce. He also started religious work in the Harris tradition as a sideline, and since his retirement from Government service in 1945 has given all his time to it. In the community, he holds the honorary position of Chief Farmer of the district. In connection with his religious work, he has adopted the title of Pastor and Superintendent-in-charge.

Mr. Nathan is very actively assisted in his work by his 'senior' (i.e. principal) wife, Sarah Emissa, a woman of about 65 years of age, and a prophetess in her own right.⁶ A native of Adwaa near Sekondi, she was, formerly, like most of her kinsfolk, a fishmonger. She is in complete control of the 'Garden' or convent at Ketan, owning the property. She declares that she had become a member of the group through divine revelation given to her in a dream. After that she went to live at the village of Busua where, for three years, she received training in the duties and the activities of a prophetess from a certain John Abrokwa, a prophet of the Twelve Apostles Church.

Although she had acquired some wealth in her previous occupation, she is now living entirely by the voluntary gifts of those who go to her for healing, supplemented with a little backyard vegetable gardening, as well as (together with her husband) on the collections taken at their religious services. The lady is an extremely vigorous and active person for her age, healthy and prosperous-looking, full of self-confidence and giving the impression of someone who is thoroughly enjoying her work. Everyone in the convent instantly obeys her, and she in turn shows great deference to her husband.

The other prominent leader of the Twelve Apostles Church is a gentleman whose headed letter paper (printed) reads as follows: 'The Twelve Apostles Orthodox Church of Ghana, Divine Faith Healing Church, Rt. Rev. Prophet Michael George, Presiding Bishop; the Reverend Henry Smith, Diocesan Secretary' (now replaced by Mr. Samuel Benn, evangelist). Bishop George is 70 years old (1958) and illiterate. He was one of the men baptized by Harris at Axim in 1914, but he came only late to leadership in the group. He used to live at Princess and it was there that, in the year 1933, he received the 'spirit.' He has been practising divine healing previously, and assisting in the Church, but from that time onward this became his principal vocation. The coming of the 'spirit' upon him was made known through the fact that one day he had a very impressive dream in which he heard a voice telling him to go to a particular place because someone there was very ill, and that if he would put his hand on this person the invalid would be restored to health. He went to the place indicated, and things turned out exactly as he had dreamt.

Bishop George has an extensive property on a lovely site lying between the main Cape Coast – Saltpond road and the sea, quite near to Saltpond. There are several dwelling houses on the land, some permanent, some temporary, providing accommodation for himself and his extended family, as well as for patients and their relations who go with them to the healing centre to take care of them. There is also a wide-open space for the healing exercises. Bishop George's cases are mostly those of mental derangement,[7] although such other ills as epilepsy, barrenness, impotence and general bodily weakness have also been brought to him for cure. It appears that the family engages in fishing as well.

The Bishop is at present building, entirely at his own expense, a chapel which is much larger and more pretentious than the one at Kadjabir. In the meantime, a cement-floored courtyard, surrounded by sheds made of palm-branches, and furnished with the usual appurtenances of a Twelve

Apostles place of worship, (cross, table with 'holy water,' etc.) serves the purposes of a chapel.

The Bishop has usually employed a clerk with the title of 'Diocesan Secretary.' The incumbent of this post in 1958 is a fine, energetic and forward-looking young man by the name of Samuel Benn. He styles himself simply 'evangelist,' and explains that his predecessor in office, who had been fond of big titles, had inserted the word 'Orthodox' into the official name of the Church without authorization, and simply because he liked the sound of it. Mr. Benn had been a stenographer-typist in Government service but had to leave because he had begun to have epileptic fits. As a Government officer he had made full use of his entitlement to free treatment in Government hospitals, then he had been to private practitioners on his own account, but had not been cured. After a number of years he had come to the Twelve Apostles for divine healing and had indeed been healed. For over three years he has had no more attacks of his distressing ailment, and feels not only generally much fitter than ever before, but is very happy as well (he is also lame in one leg). He has therefore made up his mind, as a token of his gratitude, to stay on and work for the Church in return for no more than his bare subsistence. He feels that the Church ought to be established on a firmer basis than it has at present.

Mr. Benn believes illiteracy to be the root-cause of the difficulties of the Church and thinks that if this defect could be removed, the Church would 'do wonders,' because its spiritual power, especially for healing illnesses was 'simply marvellous.' He is sure that the mission-related churches, learning what they have been missing through neglect of the 'spirit,' would benefit greatly, but he knows they would never take the Twelve Apostles Church seriously so long as its leaders remained illiterate and ignorant. It was upon his initiative that the new regulation, making literacy at least in Fanti a necessary requirement for licensing as a prophet, was made. From his views it is not surprising that he supports the recent move by the Church to seek admission in the Christian Council of Ghana.

Beliefs

The Twelve Apostles Church claims to subscribe to the same articles of faith as the major Protestant denominations in Ghana, and of the Methodist Church in particular. Mr. Nathan recalls that Prophet Harris recommended those whom he had brought away from idols to Christianity, to join the Methodist Church. The point is, however, that no importance whatsoever is attached in this Church to doctrine as such. None is taught either before or after baptism. Emphasis is laid, to the total exclusion of all other matters, upon the activity of the Holy Spirit in enabling certain men and women to predict future events, warn of impending misfortunes, detect evil-doers and, above all, to cure illnesses. Asked to put in a nutshell what their Church stood for, Mr. Nathan had no hesitation at all in exclaiming: 'We are here to heal.'

Sacred Objects

A copy of the English Bible is always prominently in evidence at all meetings whether they be for prayer and exhortation or for healing. It is not read, but placed upon the leader's table, from which it is taken to be held over the head of a candidate at baptism, and of each patient, preparatory to the healing exercises, sometimes again when the exercises are in progress.

The other sacred object in regular use is the African dancing gourd-rattle. This is a calabash with a 'neck' covered with strings of white beads. The 'neck' of the calabash serves as a handle, and the whole is rattled rhythmically to accompany singing and dancing. This instrument is used very widely in African dancing, both secular and religious. It is an essential item in the equipment of all prophets and prophetesses of the Twelve Apostles Church, and many ordinary members, including all the singers, likewise possess them. On being invited to pose for a photograph, a prophet would usually insist upon donning his white long robe of office and turban, and taking his Bible and his rattle in his left hand while holding his staff in his right. In a picture in Southon's book,[8] Harris himself is shown decked out in this way, which is doubtless how this pattern of official appearance for prophets was set. The women in the convents spend their off-duty hours making theses rattles, the while telling and embroidering stories of the wonders of healing and expulsion of evil spirits performed through the rattle, which they themselves had seen or of which they had been told by utterly reliable witness. It is firmly believed that the rattles made here are more effective in chasing away evil spirits than those procured elsewhere.

The importance of this instrument in the cult of the Twelve Apostles may be gauged by the fact that it became the centre of the most serious dispute in which the Church has ever been involved, leading to a split and even litigation. At one time the leaders of the Church wrote to the Apostolic Church of Ghana (then Gold Coast), a Pentecostal connection originating in Wales in Great Britain, and having its territorial headquarters in Accra, saying that they would welcome the financial help, supervision and leadership of foreign missionaries. They thought that this was the best mission to approach since the Apostolics also practised 'spiritual' activities. A certain Pastor J. McKeown was sent to inspect their work. He came to Kadjabir and, after observing what they did, approved of their request and, on behalf of his Mission, assumed control of their entire work. He, however, demanded that the use of the rattle should be abandoned and that it should be replaced with Western-style tambourines, and proceeded forthwith to issue these to the local groups. The leaders were greatly alarmed and thrown into confusion. Since it was in these very rattles that the power to chase evil spirits away resided, as Harris had said and experience had proved, they were not prepared to exchange them for the new article, which they regarded as a mere noise-making toy. They begged Pastor McKeown to be allowed to retain their rattles, but he would have none of them and made an issue of the matter.

In the end, his very insistence seemed to provide proof for the view, put forward by some, that what he was really after was to deprive the African prophets of spiritual power. They therefore resolved to resist him. After a period of uneasiness followed by open strife, the elders definitely cut off the new link and reverted to their former independent status. Some questions regarding property and jurisdiction had to be taken to the Magistrate's Court at Tarkwa for settlement. It appears that some leaders remained on MacKeown's side since the papers relating to the case (treasured up at Kadjabir) make no reference to Mr. Mckeown but refer to the case as 'John Bissa (substituted by Moses Andoh and others)' Plaintiff-respondents, versus John Kweku and others, Defendant-appellants.' The case took about four years (1940-43) to determine; the present leaders hired the services of a notable barrister, Lawyer Blay; and, according to Mr. Nathan, they were 'completely victorious.'

That the Twelve Apostles would still like some wider contacts is evidenced by their application in 1957 to be admitted to membership of the Christian Council of Ghana.

On one of the roof-supporting posts in the meeting place at Ketan hangs an ordinary, printed pictorial illustration – such as are commonly in use in Sunday schools – of the story of Moses striking the rock for water in the wilderness (Ex. 17). In this picture the waterpots carried by the women are of a shape similar to that of the rattles in question. This picture is used to prove and emphasize the crucial importance of this instrument in all worship if the prayers of the faithful are not to be diverted or distorted or rendered abortive through the action of evil spirits. It is taught that God himself revealed its use for this purpose for the first time when Miriam the sister of Moses took this selfsame instrument to celebrate the victorious crossing of the Red Sea.

Food Taboos

Adherents of the Twelve Apostles Church (i.e. members and others who have gone to them for healing) are not allowed to eat pork, stink-fish, shark's meat or snails. Mr. Nathan denied any Muslim influence in the prohibition of pork, saying that his has to do rather with the Gospel story of Christ and the swine which were seized by the evil spirits expelled from the demoniac. Because of their dirty habits, pigs are still a favourite resort of these spirits. Stink-fish is banned because by its smell it is unclean; the shark because it devours human flesh whenever it gets the chance, and snails because they creep through all sorts unclean places and things. The leaders are however not prepared to say whether or not these are the only unclean foods, and reserve the right to make further regulations if new revelation is received.

Smoking in any form is strictly prohibited and of alcohol only wines and beer may be taken, but never in such quantities as to produce intoxication. Opinion seems to be divided on the permissibility of palm-wine.[9]

Fasts

This church observes fasts and attaches the greatest importance to them. Mr. Nathan owns and highly recommends a pamphlet on the virtues of fasting by Franklin Hall, and says that he never tires of rereading it. Two kinds of fasts are practised: firstly the simple fast, implying abstinence from solid food until nightfall everyday for seven days at a time, and secondly the special fast in which no food – solid or liquid – may be taken at all for three days. The 'spirit' indicates to the leader which kind of fast is called for in respect of the case on hand. In serious crises the special fast may be laid upon all who happen to be living at the 'Garden' or convent at the time, or even upon the entire membership of the local group.

Social Regulations

There is no limit to the number of wives that a man may have, provided only that he is in a position to make reasonable provision for them. Whereas no divorced person may marry another in the same local congregation, there is no objection to remarriage with fellow members from other places, or with non-members. There is no compulsion on members to bring their partners in marriage into the group, though they are expected to try to win them.

For a religious group working almost exclusively among tribes which follow the rule of matrilineal descent, it is remarkable that this Church has laid down the rule that all fathers shall be responsible for the maintenance and upbringing of their children (nothing is said about nephews and nieces) up to marriage. Thereafter, the children are at liberty to join their mother's clan for all social purposes, but they must in turn assume responsibility for their father in his old age. Any person contravening this rule is warned, and if he or she persists, is expelled from the group.

Sacraments

Admission to membership of the Church is by baptism according to the peculiar rite of the sect. This consists in signing the neophyte with the mark of the Cross, in the name of the Triune God, after he or she has been thoroughly bathed and scrubbed in all parts several times over with sponge and soap. Men are bathed by men and women by women, and a minimum fee of one shilling is payable for this service. No instruction is required or given, but the new convert is encouraged to participate as much as possible in the various activities of the local group, this being regarded as fully sufficient preparation for membership.

A 'Love Feast' is held once every year, at which bread is sliced, distributed and eaten during the course of a service of worship emphasizing brotherhood and unity, both in Christ and in the work of the Church. Once or twice a year, the head of each district celebrates the sacrament of Holy Communion. There is public confession of sins, after which the leader blesses the bread and the wine, and distributes them.

Religious Practice

The centre of all religious activities is the place known in Twelve Apostles terminology as the 'Garden'. Every prophet or prophetess has a 'Garden' or is attached to one and, except in quite unusual circumstances or emergencies, operates only there. It is a sort of settlement or open convent, standing normally a little apart from other dwellings. There is a fair number of living apartments including sleeping rooms, kitchens and bathing enclosures, surrounded by vegetable gardens. Often patients who cannot find accommodation erect a hut themselves for their own use. A large 'Garden' may have as many as 30 outsiders in residence, but the usual numbers are between 10 and 20, not counting, of course, those who live in their own homes or with friends, and go to the 'Garden' at prescribed times.

In the centre of the compound is a very tall wooden cross always painted white. Every morning and at other times as required, a basinful of water is raised towards this cross three times with fervent prayer that it may be blessed by the Holy Spirit. After this ceremony the water becomes 'holy' or 'consecrated' water, efficacious for healing. It may be used at once or stored under the Cross until required.

The social centre of the community is a largish room or shed which serves both this purpose and that of place of worship. It is furnished with a table, a few chairs and African stools, and benches or other kinds of seating. A few biblical wall pictures or mottoes adorn the walls. A Bible is always on the table, often together with other books. These others are apparently placed there only in order to make a pile, for it is hard to see any other purpose that they could serve.[10] It is in this place that guests and enquirers are received, and, if the visitors are considered important, this reception may be very solemn and dignified indeed, the entire procedure of the appropriate African ceremonial being gone through with great deliberation and meticulous care. Here also is the venue for all the palavering that requires to be done.

Just before dawn every morning, and on Tuesday and Thursday evenings, as well as on Sunday mornings, services of worship are held at this place. There is little or no teaching or exposition, but the prayers are many and long, and are accompanied by sharp shrieks, deep groans and all sorts of other ejaculated interruptions, often ending in ecstatic song. The constant and almost exclusive theme of the prayers is to ask for divine help in healing. In special cases three-hourly prayer meetings are held for a prescribed number of days.

The main healing exercises are held on Fridays. The leaders explain that, since Our Lord died on a Friday, His blood, which 'heals all our diseases,' is more potently available for this work on this day of the week than on others. They point out with evident pride that they are not like the Apostolics who prohibit the use of any and all medicines. They have no objection to patent drugs or to treatment by Western-trained doctors and non-juju African herbalists. But they will not take on cases already under treatment by members of other 'spiritual' healing groups; above all they will have nothing to do with people who have gone to fetish priests with their ailments. They allege that when such people come to them and fail to confess, the 'spirit,' during the process of healing, forces them to utter a peculiar cry, whereupon they are discharged at once. Their means of cure they describe as 'only holy water and your own faith.' To the question whether, where these conditions are fulfilled, a cure is bound to result, the reply is that the Holy Spirit does not always permit this, and that it is soon revealed to a prophet if a certain case is not to be healed.

At about 8 o'clock on Friday mornings, the preparations for the healing session begin. The prophets and prophetesses don their red robes and turbans and the drummers play for a little while to alert those wishing to take part in the proceedings. The table is brought out of the meeting-place and placed under a small shed erected for the singers and drummers at one end of the open space that is to be the scene of the activities. A white tablecloth, and then the Bible and the other books are placed on the table. In front of it a wooden cross about seven feet high, covered with intertwined white and red strips of cloth, is fixed in the ground. The patients, men and women, are stripped down to the waist, made to stand facing the cross at a distance of about 20 yards or more, in lines, and are given each an enamel basin about two-thirds full of water to carry on the head. The drummers and singers then assemble under the shed. When all is ready, the leading prophet arrives, takes up his position near the table, holds up his right hand and offers a long and very hearty prayer for the blessing of the work of healing about to begin.[11] The assisting officials interrupt the prayer with many grunts of pious approval and loud ejaculations of 'Amen.' The prayer ends with the Lord's Prayer said by all together.

The drummers and singers then strike up, using rather monotonous and doleful Fanti melodies at first. However, the music gradually gets more and more agitated, and soon some of the patients begin to sway to it. When a patient makes a sudden start is the point at which the 'spirit' is believed to have hit the water. Some reach this point earlier than others; some would sink to their knees and hold out their hands in an evidently pleading posture, swaying rhythmically to the music all the time. The prophets and prophetesses move in and out among the patients, dipping their fingers in the water on their heads and gently rubbing the areas of their various complaints. Those said to be troubled by evil spirits receive gentle punches on the breast or the back, accompanied by gestures signifying expulsion.

In the meantime, the music gets 'hotter' and ever 'hotter' until it becomes a wild and almost deafening din. Incense is burned profusely and fills the air. Many patients twitch and writhe and make all sorts of the weirdest bodily contortions, spilling the water liberally over themselves and then falling on the ground and rolling over and over in the mud. The belief is that the more violently a person is shaken by the 'spirit,' the better are the prospects of a cure. It is obvious to observers that the men and the better-class women do not take on as easily as the less sophisticated women, and never quite achieve their degree of abandon. Rather they would prostrate before the cross, touching the ground with their foreheads, or clasp it with the greatest fervour and then rub their mouths in the earth before it, three times on each occasion.

A large proportion of patients are pregnant women said to be making sure of successfully delivering their babies, after having experienced a number of abortions, still births, or having lost their previous babies. Many are barren women wanting to have children. In the case of a clearly better-class young woman, evidently rather embarrassed by the proceedings but struggling hard to keep up with them (she had breasts quite undeveloped for her apparent age), a prophetess rubbed her stomach vigorously with the Bible while exorcising in very strong terms the spirit of barrenness within her. Sometimes people brought for mental disorders would, with the music, get completely out of hand, and have to be bound with ropes. On one occasion a woman rushed out from the group of patients, threw herself with great violence at the feet of a man standing among the onlookers and, clasping his feet, rubbed her mouth on the earth in front of them, wildly and many times.[12] The man (who, I was afterwards told, was her husband) lifted her up gently and handed her to one of the prophetesses, who led her away to the compound. It was explained that the 'spirit' had revealed to her that the cause of her failure to bear children was a piece of deception which she had practised on her husband, and that a cure would only be possible when she had begged for and secured his forgiveness.

The singing and drumming goes on steadily for about 3 ½ hours, with only two very short intervals. Some of the patients retire quite early, after one hour or so of the exercises. They usually end up with a final, devoted and pleading grasp of the cross. They return inside the house, take a bath, dress normally again, and often come back to the open space to view the remainder of the proceedings. Other patients continue until they are completely exhausted, and have to be carried away. Some patients join in only after the movements have been under way for a while. By about 1 o'clock p.m. all is quiet again for the week, and those not resident in the 'garden' return to their homes.

There is no secrecy whatsoever about the operations, and anybody wishing to do so may stop and watch for as long as he/she likes. Indeed it is believed that this openness to public view, with the mental discomfort that it must entail for at least some of the patients, is a not unimportant element in effecting the cure. But everyone is perfectly serious about it all, and even the strangest behaviour of the patients evokes only commiseration on the part of the onlookers, never mockery.

Asked whether the 'spirit' could also operate more quietly in individuals and under less tumultuous external conditions, Mr. Nathan expressed the view that while obviously the 'spirit' could do anything, this was apparently the way in which he chose to cure those whom trained doctors and all other available remedial resources had failed to help.

[2]

Harris' appearance was meteoric. He could have been in Ghana only a few weeks 'in the middle of 1914'[13] though it appears that, while still in the Ivory Coast, he used to send 'minor prophets' as messengers to continue what he had started. In the six years following his visit, and as a direct result of it, the Methodist Mission in the Apollonia area baptized more than 36,000 adults converted from heathenism, and in 1920 had as many as 15,000 more under catechumenical instruction.[14] But even in the Ivory Coast, which was the scene of his main activity, Harris' stay was not for long. He entered that country from his homeland of Liberia in 1913 or 1914[15], and was banished from it by the French authorities on 4th May 1915 with a strict prohibition of his re-entry on pain of imprisonment.[16] He is reported to have told the Methodist Missionary Pierre Benoit, who visited him at his home in 1926 (only three years before the Prophet's death), that he had made eight unsuccessful attempts to return to his followers in the Ivory Coast. In his own country he evoked no response whatsoever apart from mild amusement. And yet it is estimated that about 120,000 adult men and women were converted to Christianity through Harris, most of them 'receiving the sign of the Prophet' (i.e. being baptized by him), an avalanche-like movement to the Faith which has been judged to be, numerically at least, the greatest on record.[17]

With strikingly few exceptions, these converts have remained faithful to their new profession. Most have been 'gathered in' by the Methodist Mission, which was started in the Ivory Coast in 1924 expressly for this purpose (fairly recent statistics show a membership of 57,000[18] which, in view of the short time spent and the rather meager resources deployed, is indeed a very remarkable figure); some joined the Roman Catholic Church, and still others have remained Harristes (to follow M. Holas'

Frenchification), inassimilable to the Mission churches doubtless mainly because of polygamy.[19] In some districts they still outnumber all other religious groups.[20] In any case, for upwards of 40 years now 'the gods driven out have not re-appeared in the regions which (Harris) evangelized.'[21]

Our Ghanaian Twelve Apostles belong to those who have remained 'Harristes,' but they have developed along their own lines. Although they like to claim the Prophet's authority for everything that they do, it is clear that much of their present practice was evolved by their own earlier leaders. Possibly the influence of 'minor prophets' following in the wake of Harris, but with a different spirit and nothing like his gifts, such men as Bodju Ake, also played a part. However, there is no evidence that, apart from starting the custom of appointing twelve dependable men to lead each local group,[22] Harris did anything by way of organizing the churches or laying down rules and observances to regulate their life. There is no mention of 'Garden,' or fasts and food-taboos, or of 'holy water' and how it may be obtained; neither the literature on Harris himself, nor the fairly recent study (1954) by M. Holas of 'neo-harrisme' in the Ivory Coast, makes any reference to these things.

Of course the time during which Harris was permitted to work was too short, and the numbers of people with whom he was engaged during that time were far too large to allow for any such developments in organization.

It seems clear that Harris used the gourd-rattle, as the neo-harristes in the Ivory Coast use it today, and as it is in fact generally used outside this connection, merely as a musical instrument to emphasize the rhythm in singing and dancing.[23] A similar instrument is reported to be in use among some of the Nilotic tribes of Eastern Africa for purposes of divination,[24] and yet another, not very different, type of rattle is said to be operated by priests of the Ethiopian Orthodox Church with the intention of attracting the notice of saints to whom they wish to submit petitions. The same purpose is served by bells large and small, in such contexts across the world. But the ideas entertained by the Ghana Twelve Apostles concerning the gourd rattle, as sketched above, appear to be peculiarly their own.

The rationalization of the food prohibitions, the intelligibility of the preparation for baptism as well as the fact that, in Ghana generally, a great premium is placed upon fasting, would seem to indicate the same source for the eating taboos, the baptismal procedure, and the fasts observed (the use of 'holy water' is discussed elsewhere). It is particularly to be noted that the view (see page 15 above) that 'we are here to heal,' i.e. that this activity represents the major emphasis, if not indeed the exclusive preoccupation, of the group, does not derive from Harris.

That the prophet did, in fact, practise divine healing is attested by the following passage:

There has been noticed in the crowd a woman who has attempted several time to touch the cross, and held back as if she would rather not. At last she has touched it ...The woman is torn as if by a violent force. Her body is convulsed. She tears at her breasts ... At last she falls prone and rolls about in great agony. Harris goes calmly on baptizing, as if nothing were happening. After a while he goes near, and utters a strange prayer. Gradually she grows calm...She is now on her feet. This strange man again approaches the agonized soul, opens the tattered Bible and holds it before her face, the while uttering a prayer. She seems to be growing calmer now...But again she is seized by - I know not what...Harris breaks into a low laugh, turns away, and continues to baptize as before. He now approaches her for the second time, and once more holds the Bible to her face. She gradually calms down and comes to herself. She is now as helpless as a babe. She takes her seat with others of like nature and awaits baptism.[25]

Such instances must, however, have been extremely rare, or else Harris' reputation would most certainly have been for wonder-working and divine healing and not, as is actually the case, for fiery preaching against idolatry and fetishes. In circumstance where people are only too prone to credit striking personalities with such powers, it is really amazing that Harris' fame has remained what it is. This fact bears out in general, the following opinion which might seem to be slightly tinged with wishful thinking: 'Harris...does not appear to have stressed miracle, though it is said that cures of the sick were performed by him ... His aim was not physical fitness so much as a clean heart...His message formed the centre of his work.'[26]

The method of healing of the Twelve Apostles throws the main responsibility on the patient; the healers, except in cases of exorcism of evil spirits, being only assistants in the process. Patients are encouraged, and goaded on by the music, to work themselves into a state of ecstasy. Since the cure, it is held, occurs while the patient is in some degree of this state, the more fully it can be achieved, the better are the chances. It will have been noticed that several elements of the procedure are reminiscent of the case described above, in which Harris himself was involved. The big difference is, of course, that while in this case the patient was originally found in this abnormal condition (and, in fact, the cure consisted precisely in bringing her out of it), with the Twelve Apostles the condition is to be artificially induced in order that it may serve as a means of curing some other malady. In my opinion it is such cases, in which Harris afforded release to troubled minds, that, coalescing in their thoughts with traditional African views of spirit-possession and causation of illness by spirit, provided the Twelve Apostles with their pattern of a general technique for healing.

It is not only a physically exhausting, but also a mentally very hard way, at least for those who have been exposed to some school education or polished upbringing. The distress of the few such, whom I saw participating, was apparent and unmistakable. But even some simple members of the community expressed their aversion to this process because 'it is just like devil-possession.' On the other hand, that for which the Twelve Apostles are best known in their neighbourhood is their abhorrence of 'fetish.' As someone put it to me, 'the mere mention of idol or juju-medicine seems to drive them mad.' Although I was often tempted to do so, I did not have the heart to suggest to them that they were in fact using the Bible as a sort of juju or fetish.

NOTES

[1] Vide A.E. Southon, More King's Servants (Atlantis Press) pp. 97, 110.
There are several books and articles on Harris and his movement. A list of them is given at p. 241f. of Katesa Schlosser, Propheten in Afrika; another list is in B. Holas, 'Bref Aperçu sur les principaux Cultes Syncrétiques de la Basse Cote d' Ivoire,' in Africa vol. XXIV, 1 (January 1954); to the works there mentioned may be added: T. Fenton, Black Harvest.

[2] A seven man committee now regulates district affairs, local groups are usually headed each by one man or woman only.

[3] In matrilineal Akan society, the nephew takes the place of son and heir. It is reported that some prophets consecrated their relatives to that office even though these did not possess any of the necessary gifts and powers.

[4] See Appendix A.

[5] This is probably being done by Mr. Nathan, possibly with the assistance of Mr. Benn. They appear to be the only persons in the sect capable of making such an undertaking. In a discussion on the necessity of education, an illiterate prophet made the point that reliance should be upon the 'spirit' and not 'book-learning,' but he was silenced by being asked whether Mr. Nathan (i.e. literate) did not have the 'spirit.'

[6] Katesa Schlosser, Propheten in Afrika, p. 248, reports that Harris constantly had the companionship of two or three women who operated the gourd-rattle to beat the tact for the singing. Without further evidence (which is lacking) it cannot be assumed, however, as she does, that they were his wives. At least with our Twelve Apostles quite a few would-be prophetesses hang around and render all sorts of minor service without having marital relationships with the prophets.

[7] When I visited this place there were three persons suffering from mental disorders; a man, a woman, and a boy. The woman was held in chains. I was told that the less serious cases remained in their own homes, but altogether about ten were receiving treatment.

THE CHURCH OF THE TWELVE APOSTLES 25

[8] See first reference in Note 1 above.
[9] Whereas Mr. Nathan (doubtless as a result of his Methodist background and early training (was evidently disgusted at the suggestion and said that it would be 'a big disgrace' for a prophet to partake of it, another prophet present quietly said: 'I drink it and it is very good.' Thereupon a lively argument took place, in the course of which several made the point that since Christ permitted the use of palm branches at his triumphal entry into Jerusalem, there could be nothing wrong with drinking the wine of the same palm. This view seemed to prevail.
[10] On one occasion there were a dictionary, a school reader, a book on geography, and a couple of the volumes widely distributed, usually free of charge, by 'Jehovah's Witnesses' colporteurs.
[11] I felt the greatest admiration for a prayer offered once by Bishop George. It had all the intimacy and the tone of assurance regarding the presence of the addressee which characterize prayers said at family libations, while for eloquence, cogency and the logical sequence of the thoughts I considered it was superb.
[12] This act is well known, especially among the Akans, as a sign of repentance and pleading for forgiveness when an inferior has offended a superior, or as a sign of utter submission.
[13] Katesa Schlosser, *Propheten in Afrika*, p. 244.
[14] Katesa Schlosser, *Propheten in Afrika*, p. 265.
[15] Katesa Schlosser, *Propheten in Afrika*, p. 244.
[16] Thomas Fenton, *Black Harvest*, p. 69f.
[17] Katesa Schlosser, *Propheten in Afrika*, p. 257, 263
[18] Thomas Fenton, *Black Harvest*, p. 131.
[19] Thomas Fenton, *Black Harvest*, p. 107.
[20] B. Holas, '*Bref Aperçu sur les Principaux Cultes Syncrétiques de la Basse Côte d'Ivoire*, *Afrika* vol. XXIV, 1 (January 1954), pp. 55-60.
[21] B. Holas, '*Bref* Aperçu *sur les Principaux Cultes Syncrétiques de la Basse Côte d'Ivoire*, *Afrika* vol. XXIV, 1 (January 1954), pp. 55-60.
[22] This practice is no longer observed in Ghana: see p. 9 and Note 2 above thereto.
[23] W. J. Platt, *An African Prophet*, p. 59, quoting from Marty, '*Etudes sur L'Islam en Côte d' Ivoire*,' ... a calabash, containing dried seeds, which he shakes to keep rhythm for his hymns.' See also the article by B. Holas referred to above.
[24] H. Des champs, Les Religions de l' Afrique Noire, p. 63.
[25] W. J. Platt, *An African Prophet*, p. 56f, quoting from 'One of (Harris') African contemporaries, a barrister-at-law.'
[26] W. J. Platt, *An African Prophet*, p. 59. 'The belief of the prophet, according to M. Marty, could be summed up in four articles: Belief in One God, the abandoning and destroyed of fetishes, the observance of the Sunday·rest, prohibition of adultery with maintenance of polygamy. This creed accepted, the people were baptized.' A rather fuller account of Harris' teaching is given by B. Holas in his article cited above: (My own translation) "The essential traits of his mission can be summed up in a few words: a pitiless fight against the "fetishes," followed by their destruction; exorcism and annihilation of "sorcerers;" condemnation of lying, thieving, drunkenness, adultery; the threat to hell to sinners and promise of a reward for the righteous in paradise; forgiveness of sins through baptism; toleration of certain customary institutions, particularly polygamy; obedience to superiors and the administrative authorities; and finally a sympathetic attitude towards the Christian churches.' Katesa Schlosser, *Propheten in Afrika*, p. 249 (my own translation): 'As far as Walker was able to ascertain, Harris spoke little of Christ except that he died on the cross for mankind. No one could remember hearing Harris speak of the miracles of Jesus or of his teaching.'

CHAPTER THREE

The Musama Disco Christo Church

[1]

FOR this story of the movement my sources are the oral reports given at my meetings with the leaders at Mazano, as well as two written documents: the first a brief history of the Church published in Fanti by the founder himself (Fanzaar Press, Koforidua, 1943; English title, Musama Disco Christo Church History); the other a longer history by a senior priest of the Church, the Rev. B. E. Yorke. It is also written in Fanti, and is as yet in manuscript. The Akaboha, who very graciously let me have it for several weeks, told me that there were mistakes in it, but that after these had been corrected the manuscript would be published as the Church's official history. I had some difficulty in reconciling incidents or dates here and there: in such cases my order of preference was 1. The founder's history (he gives the impression of having been a precise man who kept written notes of events); 2. The oral reports given me at Mazano; and 3. Yorke's history.

Joseph William Egyanka Appiah, afterwards known as Prophet Jemisemiham Jehu-Appiah, Akaboha I, was born 'two years before the Prempeh War,' that is, in 1893. He was a native of Abura Edumfa in the Central Province of the Gold Coast (now Ghana). His father was member of the Twida tribe and was called Kwaa Dum while his mother, Abena Esuon, belonged to the Adwenadze tribe. They had four sons and three daughters: Kobina Gyan, Abena Asawa, Yaa Oboo, Efua Maansa, Kofi Appiah (who became the prophet), Kweku Kwaesar and Kweku Wudi. They were Methodist.

Five days after Appiah's birth an unknown stranger, passing through the village, prophesied that the boy would one day become a great messenger of God, and strongly advised that he should be sent to school when he grew up. At the age of eight years his older brother Kobina Gyan sent him to the Methodist village school at Abura Dunkwa. Their father was not convinced of the necessity of school education and took no interest in the matter.

At school Appiah was very popular because he had a jovial nature and was always full of fun. He particularly enjoyed Sunday School and was a very keen member of the local church choir. For this reason he was well liked by all the ministers who successively took charge of the congregation. Later he transferred to Cape Coast to continue his education, and finished elementary school there at the age of eighteen years.

The Methodist superintendent minister of his home circuit, the Rev. Mr. Stanhope, appointed him a teacher at the village school of Abakrampa-Dunkwa and when, a short time afterwards, the headmaster and catechist-in-charge of the mission station died, Appiah was promoted to that position. He worked at Abakrampa for three years, during which time he married a woman called Abena Nomaa. They had three children.

In those days the pay of a village catechist was very meagre and Appiah, unable to make ends meet, abandoned teaching and preaching to become a cocoa broker. He went to the Akyem Abuakwa district which at that time was enjoying a great boom in the cocoa industry. This venture proved a complete failure. Appiah returned to his home district and spent sometime at Agona Abodom, trying his hand at several odd jobs one after the other, but was no more successful than before. While there the new Methodist circuit superintendent, the Rev. Ernest Bruce, heard of him and offered him re-employment as a teacher-catechist at Gomoa Dunkwa.

Samuel Nyankson

During his stay at this place, Appiah was greatly impressed by the activities of a 'Prophet' by the name of Samuel Nyankson. He was a divine healer who, apart from curing many illnesses by supernatural means, also performed other miracles. On one occasion, when a heavy forest tree was about to fall on some huts in a village, Nyankson stopped it from coming down completely by merely placing his walking-stick under it. The villagers were thereby enabled to clear the huts; but even when the tree finally came to the ground, it did not fall on the huts, but in an open space nearby, although this had not been in the original direction of the fall of the tree. Also Prophet Nyankson, by prayer, caused the body of a youth who had been drowned in the Offin River to come up after the bereaved family had searched for it five days but in vain. Again, in the prophet's old age, one day when he desired very much to drink coconut milk, he earnestly entreated God to pluck the nuts for him. A great wind then blew and shook down as many nuts as he wanted.

This holy man spent many years at Ashanti Gyakobu in the Dunkwa - Offin area, and returned to his own home district of Onyaa-wonsu only when he was already an old man and nearly blind. He remained a Methodist catechist throughout his active years and never attempted to found his own church. Appiah held him in profound veneration, and often said that he wished to God he could have the Holy Spirit as Nyankson did.

The Call of the Prophet

While at Gomoa Dunkwa, Appiah was denounced to the circuit superintendent, the Rev. Mr. Assan at Apaa, for practising curious magical rites and customs, and indulging in the use of secret medicine and special drugs obtained from India and America. Mr. Assan went into the matter but saw no reason to take disciplinary action of any kind, and Appiah was left alone. He had in fact begun to keep fasts. During one of these, one day, as he was reclining in an easy chair and meditating on spiritual things, he fell into a trance. He saw three angels descending from heaven and holding a crown which, when they came to him, they placed on his head. They removed it again and repeated this action three times, after which they returned to heaven, taking the crown back with them. Appiah was greatly surprised and wondered what this vision could mean.

While he was reflecting upon the matter, he received a call from Job Cartey, a pupil and co-worker of Samuel Nyankson. He was also a 'spiritual' man. The first thing which Cartey said on his arrival was this: 'Master Appiah, God has made you a great king. On my way here I saw you in a vision dressed like a king, with a crown on your head, and angels were bringing you down to the earth from heaven. In this way God sends me to tell you that he has made you a great king.'

Cartey then asked Appiah if he had prepared a special place in the open for prayer. The answer being in the negative, he sent for the leading members of Appiah's congregation and showed them how to prepare such a place. He told them to take good care of their catechist because he was a man of God, full of the Holy Spirit. The people went to work on the chosen site that very day, and in the evening all were able to assemble there and offer their prayers to God. Many among them received the Holy Spirit after Job Cartey had laid his hand upon them and blessed them, and all promised from that time onward to do the work of God. This place of prayer is called the 'camp.'

On the 18th of August 1919, when Appiah was praying in the 'camp,' he heard a noise as of a great crowd of people singing and praising God. As he listened the Angel of the Lord revealed himself to him, coming towards him with a Bible in his hand, opened at the 10th chapter of the

Book of Acts of the Apostles, and pointing out this chapter to him. Then God's Spirit descended upon Appiah. When this revelation was ended, Appiah realized that he had become a new man. He began to speak in a new tongue, and from that time onward he performed many miracles.

The Miracles of Prophet Appiah

The first miracle happened when the prophet visited a very sick person near Gomoa Dunkwa. (This village, which used to be called Gomoa Swedru, has now been completely abandoned, and is 'gone back to bush.') The man had been so seriously ill that his death was believed to be imminent, but he was healed instantaneously after prayer and laying on of hands by the prophet; and so completely was his health restored that he was even able to accompany the prophet a considerable way when he left again.

Most of Prophet Appiah's miracles were those of healing, and they were accomplished by fervent prayer; but on one occasion, when returning from the prayer camp with his followers, his attention was called to a poisonous snake creeping near where they were. Appiah quickly pointed at the serpent with his walking-stick, whereupon it stood quite still. When, after a while, the men ventured to approach the creature with sticks, intending to kill it, they found to their utter amazement that it was already dead.

Years latter, after Appiah had founded his own church, his younger brother, Joseph Odum, died. He was the first member of the new church to die. Appiah prayed over him until he was restored to life. Odum finally died about one year afterwards, of a quite different illness. This happened at Onyaawonsu.

Transfer to Gomoa Oguan

From the time that Appiah knew he was a prophet, he began to retreat more and more for prayer and meditation, and he formed a special prayer group within the local congregation. On 9th May 1920 his Church authorities moved him to a more important station, Gomoa Oguan, the capital of the paramount chief of the entire Gomoa tribe. At that time the paramount chief was Nana Kodwo Nkum. The Church members at Oguan had heard about Appiah and asked him many questions concerning the Holy Spirit, but he did not answer, because he was afraid.

Hannah Barnes

About the end of May 1920, some three weeks after Appiah's removal to Oguan, he admitted to his prayer group a young woman by the name of Abena Baawa, whom he renamed Hannah Barnes. She was a native of Oguan and belonged to the Aboaradze tribe. She and her elder sisters were keen members of the local congregation and of its singing band though their parents were pagan. However, Hannah never held any position of leadership in the church. In Appiah's group she soon distinguished herself because of her 'spiritual' activities, and came to be looked upon as second only to Appiah himself for 'spiritual' power. One day she fell into a trance and for five hours lay as one dead. When he regained consciousness she told her friends who, surrounding her, had been praying for her all that time, that in her trance she had seen a great ladder reaching from earth to heaven. An angel came down the ladder with an open Bible in his right hand. He stretched the Bible towards her and said to her: 'with this Bible I send you together with Catechist Appiah to carry the Word to all the nations of the earth. You shall be the helper and daughter of the teacher in my name. Do not be afraid.' The group was greatly encouraged by what Hannah said, and continued praying fervently until the time for dispersal.

The Three 'Baptisms' of the Prophet Appiah

On one occasion Hannah fasted for seven days, and throughout this time the 'Holy Spirit' was upon her. At night an angel gave her some white food to eat. Instead of being weakened, she was rather exceedingly strengthened by her fast, and was able to do many wonderful things. She could tell who were evil persons, and those upon whom some disaster or misfortune was about to fall. God informed the group through her that he was going to give the prophet Appiah a special baptism. Five members of the group were selected to be witnesses. On the appointed day they foregathered and began to pray at about nine o'clock of the evening. Towards midnight Hannah suddenly shouted that the seven angels were coming, and at that very moment a strange liquid poured down straight from heaven on to Appiah's head, wetting his clothes. The liquid was fragrant beyond description and tasted sweater than honey. Then God spoke to Appiah through Hannah and said that this holy baptism, which he would give him three times, was the sign that Appiah was specially consecrated for the work of God; he should fear nothing, for God had created him and Hannah just for this purpose; he would make Appiah a great king of men.

When Appiah had heard these words, the 'Holy Spirit' came upon him and he spoke in 'tongues.' The group joyfully praised God for showing them such wonderful things. However, when Hannah announced that God would take Appiah up into heaven for three months, they pleaded hard in prayer that no such thing should happen, as they would need to account for his absence to his people. God heard their cries and supplications, for the town was the capital of the Gomoa state, and he granted their request.

The second baptism took place on Sunday the 20th of March 1922. The members of the group had been told to cleanse and prepare themselves by fasting and prayer. The message delivered to Appiah through Hannah was this: 'Today I have given you power over evil spirits. You will heal many possessed of evil spirits, and do many other wonders which will surprise even yourself.' The members of the group were so happy about all that had happened that they continued singing and praying throughout the night until dawn.

On Friday 7th March 1924 the members, at that time numbering 115 in all, assembled at an appointed place for the third and final baptism of the prophet. It was a sight worthy of being seen. The 'Holy Spirit' came upon the whole group, and some were so full of it that they had to be carried home. From that time onward Appiah and Hannah were given the titles of Akaboha and Akatitibi respectively, honorific names revealed from heaven to distinguish them as the undoubted leaders appointed by God. All the members became firm in the faith, and were fully convinced that, however hard life might become, they would remain undaunted.

The Two Ascensions of the Queen

One day God revealed to Hannah that he would take her to heaven and crown her there for her glorious deeds. She informed her friends who decided to pray God not to do this. While they were still praying, Hannah suddenly disappeared from their midst. That was at about eight o'clock in the evening. The group was greatly troubled, not knowing what to say to her relatives after the meeting. So they resolved to continue praying and to wait. At about eleven o'clock, while they were still praying, they were startled by three gunshots and a great light which suddenly shone upon them. All took to their heels except Appiah and a woman by the name of Joanna, who remained steadfast. When they opened their eyes, there was Hannah lying in front of them. They took hold of her and held her fast for fear she might vanish again, and called the others. They asked Hannah where she had been, and she told them that the seven angels had carried her into heaven where she had been crowned a queen. They were therefore from that time on to call her Nathalomoa, which was the heavenly word for 'Queenmother.' The angels had told her that God had given her to Appiah to aid him in his spiritual work; that is was in order to find her that he had been made to come to Oguan, for it was to be throw and her together that wonders would be done for the salvation of the people. The light which the group had seen was the glory of the angels who brought her back to earth from heaven, and the gunshots were their signs.

On Good Friday in 1922, Nathalomoa indicated that God would take her into heaven a second time. The 'Spirit' remained on her very strongly throughout that day and the next. The members, not wanting her to be taken away again, kept strict watch over her, and even refused to meet at their usual place for prayer. Instead they assembled in Appiah's sitting-room and locked the door. They advised the Queen to relax a little in her spiritual thought so that she might not be carried away, but she only smiled. At about eight o'clock, she shouted that the angels were coming, and soon after that she vanished from their midst. They were all so surprised that they did not know what to do. As the people did not believe in any of their 'spiritual' works, they realized that there would be great trouble unless the Queen was found again, so they searched for her until Sunday morning but in vain. No morning service was held that day. In the early afternoon while Appiah, exhausted, was resting in his easy chair, he dreamt that the members were circling the church with singing, he himself was scattering corn and the Queen was following him. When he awoke, he had the church bell rung to call the members together, and told them that they should do as he had dreamt. After marching around the church three times with songs, they hopefully entered it, and indeed the Queen, was there lying in the pulpit. Appiah ran and seized her and held her high, and there was great jubilation.

The Queen was taken home and asked what had happened. She said she did not know, but that suddenly she had found herself in the kingdom of heaven. There was an atmosphere of holiness about the whole place; the houses were built with glass and were surrounded by the most lovely and sweet-smelling flowers; it was quite easy to see objects in the interiors of houses even at great distances. The angels showed her round many important places, but what surprised her most was that with one step you could cover about two miles. At the end of the sightseeing they were passed by a great procession of angels in which a man was being carried shoulder high. The angels asked her if she knew him, and she said that she did not. They told her that was the man who would become lord over the new church which was being established. If the members would receive him wholeheartedly, they would be free from all ills and want for nothing. He would be born on earth through herself the Queen and the prophet Appiah, so the members should pray earnestly for the time of his birth. After that the angels said they would return her to earth as her friends were bewailing her disappearance and so, although she herself would have much preferred to stay on in heaven, she suddenly found herself in the pulpit, not having the slightest idea as to just how she got there. The people upon hearing this, greatly rejoiced and gave thanks to God, and determined to hold fast to the new faith. At that time the Queen was as yet unmarried.

Appiah's Dismissal from the Service of the Methodist Church
During 1923 the Rev. Gaddiel Acquaah, then the circuit superintendent, firmly ordered Appiah to stop all his occult practices completely and at once, 'as the Methodists were not like that.' Since the prophet was unable to obey this order, he was dismissed from the service. People who knew him came from many places to sympathize with him and to console him, and they greatly encouraged him to continue his 'spiritual' work for the good of all. He removed from the Mission station but did not leave the town as the paramount chief was willing for him to stay on under his protection. This he did because Appiah had, by instantaneous divine healing, restored the health of the chief's senior wife, who had been paralysed for a long time.

At that time, the difference of opinion about the prophet within the Methodist local congregation had become extremely acute. On Christmas Eve in 1923, during the Chief's absence at Winneba, the townspeople, both Christians and heathen, were summoned together by means of war drums. With much shouting, threatening and gun-firing, they stormed the 'camp' and destroyed it, cutting into pieces the bamboo sticks which supported the shed. No one was hurt, but one man, who asked the aggressors why they were doing this, and tried to stop them, was beaten and dragged on the ground.

Under a deep sense of persecution which, however, merely increased their determination to stand fast, and their unity among themselves, Appiah and his followers left Gomoa Oguan and went to Onyaa-Wonsu. Here, directed by a vision, Appiah asked for the hand of Hannah Barnes, Nathalomoa, in marriage, and the proposal was gladly approved by her parents. The betrothed couple fasted for three months and seven days, during which time they ate only in the evenings and then very sparingly, so that blessing might come upon all that they would do. About that time the prophet's new name of Jemisemiham Jehu-Appiah was revealed to him from above.

The Founding of the Musama Disco Christo Church
On Thursday 19th October 1922 Appiah and a number of his friends met at Oguan. They decided to call themselves Egyidifu Kuw (meaning 'Faith Society') and to meet regularly every Thursday 'in order to seek the Holy Spirit as the Apostle did.' There were five prophets among them, and their activities included prayer, healing, and speaking in 'tongues.' The main subjects of their supplications were 'victory' for their group, power to do wonders, and the welfare of the members. This group with changing membership has since met regularly every Thursday without interruption

until the present day. At a camp meeting once the official name for the society was revealed from heaven at Musama Disco Christo Church, which means the Army of the Cross of Christ Church. In May 1925 a seven-day conference was held, during which the prophet and his wife were again acknowledged as the undisputed leaders of the society, and set apart as its full-time workers. A 'covenant' was made, by which the members engaged themselves to abstain from drumming and dancing with their Asafo companies (i.e. clan groups), working on Fridays, giving any contribution towards the performance of fetish customs or partaking in Ahoba and other heathen rites, ceremonies and festivals.

The keeping of the new regulations soon brought the group into conflict with the townspeople of Onyaawonsu. Friday was the day for doing communal service and, although the group pleaded to be allowed to do its share of the work on any other day of the week, the townspeople of Onyaawonsu insisted that they should work together with everybody else. The situation became quite unbearable and so, for the sum of £37/10/-, the group acquired from the Chief of Fomena Gomoa a site near Gomoa Abodom for a settlement of their own, and cleared the dense forest by their own labour.

The removal to the new site was planned and carried out in such a manner as to be reminiscent of the Exodus of the Israelites from Egypt. There was much preparation consisting mainly of fasting, special prayer services and ceremonial washings. It was then that the rite of Inaabi, or rosary prayers peculiar to this group, was introduced. The final procession from Onyaawonsu to the new place, which occurred on 17th October 1925, was carried out with great rejoicing, 'like the Israelites after passing through the Red Sea.' An angel revealed the name of the new place as Mazano, which is a heavenly word meaning 'my own town.' Those who took part in this event were afterwards known as the 'Jehunano Family,' meaning 'Companions or Followers of Jehu,' and are looked upon as the foundation member of the new church. Whereas previously the prophet Jehu used to convert pagans and to send them to join their own choice, from now on he admitted them into his own church.

At Mazano further organization and a grading of the workers took place. This, however, resulted in a split led by one Samuel Dankwa, who was dissatisfied with the grade to which he had been assigned, and, after quarrelling with the leader, severed his connection with the church and went away, taking three other prophets with him. Nine prophets still remained, including Jehu himself.

The Birth of Matapoly Moses Jehu-Appiah

The son who had been promised to Prophet Jehu and Nathalomoa when they were at Oguan was born to them at Onyaawonsu on 24th August 1924, which was a Sunday. The people were praying in 'camp' at the time. As this child was born 'in the spirit,' the water in which he was bathed became a very potent medicine for curing sterility in women, and septic sores. Even his napkins were used for healing many diverse diseases, and other wonderful things happened at the time of his birth. The moon assumed the colour of blood, cocoa seeds were found hanging on cornstalks and cobs of corn were found on trees and mushrooms. These strange things happened because indeed a wonderful child had been born. In the evening of the same day the child was brought before God to be given a heavenly name and he was called Matapoly Moses. His common, earthly name was Kwesi Nyamekye, i.e. 'Sunday-born Godsent.'

On 1st September 1924 the Queenmother received the following message from God: 'Bless the Reverend Funamafubu Adoo Eshun and his wife Kupabinaia Eshun and say to them that, because of their good services to God, they would become the parent of the wife of Matapoly Moses. You should all be united in everything and pray steadfastly for this thing to happen.' This was announced to all the people, who rejoice greatly to hear it, and went about singing songs of joy to and carrying palm branches in their hands. They decided to offer sacrifices for this child once in every three months.

The 'wife' of Matapoly Moses was duly born on 1st September 1925, also at the time of prayer in the 'camp', just when the quarterly sacrifices for the birth of Matapoly were being offered. He was bathed immediately, so that his bathe water might be used for bathing the new-born girl. The heavenly name which she received was Matabinaia. Many miracles were performed at the time of her birth.

'Peaceful Year' Celebration

Matapoly's first birthday was celebrated with great rejoicing. During the festival, God spoke to the people through Prophet Jehu about the peace which had come to mankind through the resurrection of Jesus Christ. Further, he commanded that when this time came (i.e. the anniversary of Matapoly's birth) all the people of the new church should gather to celebrate it as a great festival. They should play drums and musical instruments and praise God as the Israelites had done, with singing and dancing, and should exchange presents among themselves, as was the custom at Christmas. This celebration should last seventeen days, it should be known as the 'Peaceful Year' or Asomdwee Afi festival, and be regarded as the church's most important feast of the year. If kept with enthusiasm it would secure or the members remission of Divine punishment and rest, peace and blessing for the ensuing year. The people thereupon held a procession through the town, and have kept the custom of this feast (upon a much bigger scale, of course) ever since.

It was upon this occasion of the celebration of Matapoly's first birthday that the new church's own bell was rung for the first time. Prophet Jehu declared that the days of unpopularity, persecution and fear, when the members had to hold their meetings in private, summoning one another by means of secret signs, had definitely and finally come to an end, and that thenceforward they would be able to function openly.

The Spread of the Church

When the people first moved to Mazano, they each received a heavenly name. They devoted themselves to prayer and the invocation of spirits, doing no other spirit-invocation work besides. They had audiences with God continually, and he promised them a great new church with power to heal all illnesses and to foretell the future. For this reason they did not return to their various towns, but waited at Mazano patiently for the fulfilment of these promises. At this time Prophet Jehu started celebrating himself the sacrament of Holy Communion, thus cutting off the last links with the Methodist Church.

On 29th August 1929 God through the prophet Jehu, summoned all the people to the 'camp' and prescribed a 'system' for them in preparation for the great work that he intended them to do. They were to withdraw from all contacts with other people for seven days, and then 'fast' (eating only in the evenings and sparingly) and pray for three weeks. After this, for a rest, they should return to normal living for three days, and then repeat the whole process all over again. This was done throughout one entire year. At the end of it, God revealed the day on which the new church was to launch out into all the world to 'beat gong-gong about God' (bo Onyame ho dawura, i.e. proclaim God). That day was the 9th September 1930, and upon it Prophet Jehu and his followers set out to preach and to warn the towns and villages to which they went of future happenings. Their sermons dealt mainly with the nearness of doomsday, the signs of its approach and the terrible fate, after the Judgment, of all evildoers: adulterers, idolaters, murderers, all men of violence, and those who practised witchcraft. The signs would be the outbreak of all sorts of disease epidemics, the turning of the sky to blood-red colour, and the sudden appearance at mid-day of a great, black rain-cloud. When these things came to pass, all good people able to do so should flee to Mazano, where they would be told what to do; others should immediately assemble in the middle of whatever town or village they might find themselves in at the time, and pray to God publicly and fervently for the disaster to be turned away. In the meantime, all fetishes and charms of all kinds should be burnt.

As a result of this preaching, many people came to join the new church, and local congregations were formed at Abura Edumfa, Edwumako Afransi and elsewhere. A prophet, teacher, or healer was appointed to lead each of these groups. The converts were particularly impressed by the fact that, upon the admission of each new member into the church, the Holy Spirit would reveal to Prophet Appiah the name by which God wished him or her to be known. In this way over four thousand people received new names, each a different one. This was very wonderful.

Soon afterwards the prophet established Miniodzupa, where he trained prophets and priest, an Alishidani where he trained teachers and healers. He taught them how to hold the Inaabi (rosary) prayers, and wrote orders of service for Sunday morning worship, holy marriage, the celebration of the sacraments, burial of the dead, ordination to the priesthood, the naming ceremony, and all other church occasions. Above all the taught his followers how one presents oneself to God and gains audience with him. Prophet Appiah also wrote a history of his Church.

In the year 1945 God informed the Prophet that he had only two more years to live, so he should set his house in order. When the Synod of 1947 was held, he announced publicly that, having served the Church for 25 years he had finished his work. Many people attend synod on this occasion, and received the 'water of life.' The death of old Job Cartey Alibunabi, a prominent leader in the Church, took place at this time. Soon afterwards, Prophet Appiah embarked upon his 'Victorious Journey,' which had been prophesied many years before.

The 'Victorious Journey'

The Prophet first went to Cape Coast where he gave a party to celebrate the 25 years' Jubilee of his Church. He was accompanied by the choir of singers and seven horn-blowers who heralded his arrival in every town. Everywhere he went he was most cordially welcomed. He visited Apam, Winneba (where his party was presided over by Nana Ghartey, the Paramount Chief of the State), Agona Kwanyako, and Nyaakrom. Form there he proceeded to Accra, and crossed the Volta to Akwamu, finally ending up at Koforidua. Everywhere ther theme of his addresses was the same: he had done the work which God had given him to do, and was now leaving a sound and growing church in the hands of the elders. He spent altogether 2 ½ months on these travels, and returned home quite exhausted.

On 19th March 1948, he was summoned to a conference of the Aborigines' Rights Protection Society at Cape Coast. He had been a member of the Society for many years and, for sometime, was on its Executive Committee; however, on one occasion, he had prophesied that although freedom and independence would come to the Gold Coast, this would not happen through the Society. On the occasion of this visit to Cape Coast, the Prophet stopped at Saltpond to hold a consultation with Dr. Kwame Nkrumah on the question of the restoration of peace and good order in the country, after the big riots of the beginning of 1948.

While stopping at Saltpond, the Prophet received an urgent call from a woman to come to her daughter who was in labour; she had been at the hospital but her people had been told that her condition was hopeless and she had been returned home. Though the Prophet was in a hurry to continue his journey, he went to them and, placing his hand upon the woman's head, offered a fervent prayer to God for her deliverance. Thereupon, to the utter amazement of all, the baby was quietly and safely born. Though the people would have liked him to stay a little longer, he took leave of them and went on to his meeting. This was very successful, and there too the elders asked him to pray for the success of the Society's affairs.

At the following Seenim meeting, and all subsequent church meetings in which he spoke, the Prophet made farewell speeches, urging his people to hold together, to be loyal to the Church, and to try to spread it far and wide. In his preparation for the approaching synod, he fasted for seven days, during which time many secrets were revealed to him, and in visions he saw both those who in the past had tried to do away with him, and those who were still plotting the ruin of the Church.

Two prominent members who had taken a disagreement to the civil authorities for settlement, instead of thrashing it out within the Church as was the Musama custom, he expelled from the Church. He called his household with his twelve children together in the presence of leaders of the Church, and strongly exhorted them to remain united as a family. For Matapoly Moses (second son, present Akaboha) he had these special words: 'You, my son, are quite different from the rest; I gave you the training befitting your rank, and now that his period of preparation is over, put away childish things and become a man. Take good and proper care of all my affairs.' In the same way he had meetings with various groups of his prophets, priest and healers, discussing he welfare of the Church and invoking the 'Spirit' with them, and showing them how to keep strong in spiritual matters.

The following 'Peaceful Year' celebration started on 24th August 1948. On the following day the Prophet, arrayed in his richest vestments, welcomed the assembly and blessed all present. In his address he stated that he was victorious because God had fulfilled all this promises to him.

However, the people appeared very subdued and sad, because they did not like the way he looked, thin and different from his old self. From the third day of the festival onward he was no longer able to attend any sessions, but the conference carried on as usual, under the leadership of his lieutenants. The proceedings were finally brought to an end by the reading and exposition of Phil. 4. 9 with reference to the Prophet. The latter was extremely pleased to see that the members were not discouraged by his inability to be with them, and gave thanks to God because he felt convinced that the Church would survive his own death and continue to flourish.

Death of the Prophet

On 23rd September 1948, at ten o'clock in the morning, Prophet Appiah breathed his last. He received the burial of a king, for such he was. Even during his lifetime there were many who never referred to him except as King Jehu Akaboha I. He was buried at Old Mazano, but when his people moved from there to resettle at New Mazano they, with the permission of the Government and under the supervision of the Government Medical Department, exhumed his body and brought it with them to their new dwelling place where it now rest finally at the very centre of the town.

The 'Heavenly Baptism' of Akaboha II

All the members of the Church present at Mazano fasted three days. At noon on each of these days, Matapoly Moses was anointed by his mother the Queenmother. On the third day, Saturday the 9th of November 1948, at about nine o'clock pm, all the people assembled around a dais upon which the late Prophet Appiah's chosen son had taken his place. Throughout that day, prayers and spiritual invocations were held at half-hourly intervals. At about midnight the Queenmother, being in the spirit, announced to the gathering that she saw angels coming to the place where they were. As the people looked up, everybody saw a crystal ball the size of an ordinary football, descending gently from heaven. It lighted on Matapoly's head and broke, wetting him and his clothes completely from head to feet. The spray from the splash even reached some of the members standing near the dais.

A deafening cry of jubilation went up from the crowd; in fact, none of those present will ever forget this wonderful occasion. As the dais was cemented, many people rushed to collect this heavenly water, the surpassingly sweet fragrance of which filled the whole atmosphere. The 'heavenly water' collected by those fortunate ones who managed to get some was used for healing with wonderful effect. When the clothes of the new Akaboha were washed, the wash-water was shared out to be used in healing, and some of it is still available.¹ If kept in a bottle and used sparingly, this miraculous water has the power of filling up the bottle again by itself.

In those days many people in dreams and visions saw Akaboha I walking happily in the company of angels.

[2]

In 1958 this Church claimed 150 local branches throughout all the Regions of Ghana excepting the Northern Region, and a total membership of 18,000: approximately 6,000 children and youths, 7,000 adult female and 5,000 adult male, members.[2] These estimates were stated to be based on the records of the central office which, however, were not available for study. The Head of the Church estimated that about 30 per cent of the members had been converted from paganism whereas the rest were former members of the historic Christian churches. The local branches are grouped into 13 'circuits,' each under the supervision of a superintendent minister.[3] There are also scattered members in French Togoland, Nigeria, and as far afield as Liberia, though the group which had spontaneously organized itself in Nigeria had had to be disowned owing to its introduction new doctrine of an occult nature.[4]

Teaching

An official summary of the Church's doctrines is reproduced as Appendix B 1. It is, however, necessary to amplify this statement by drawing attention to the following significant facts:

1. The two Testaments of the Bible are regarded as having equal authority. It is reported that the founder of the Church repeatedly declared that God had said to him: 'Why do some of my messengers believe in the Old Covenant and not in the New? Why do some believe in the New but not in the Old? I am the same God who speaks in the Old Testament as in the New.' This declaration is usually quoted to justify the Ark, sacrifices, polygamy, Levitical rules of purification, statements about angels and demons, etc.

2. The MDCC has its own version of the Apostles' Creed. This inserts the name of the Church, thus: '... I believe in the Holy Ghost, the holy Musama Disco Christo Church and all true Christian churches everywhere in the world, the communion of saints ...'

3. The MDCC forbids all participation in customs performed in respect of ancestors, including the keeping of the traditional annual festival (called Ahoba in its home area); all fetish worship or consultation or mediums, sorcerers, invokers of spirits, and Muslims; all amulets, charms, and talismans or any 'juju' protection against witches or any other evil.

4. The MDCC does not merely 'believe in Divine Healing' (art. 13). Its stand is more accurately described by an older statement of this article: 'Let no one avoid the holy healing and take medicine for the healing of disease.'

5. This Church has a rich and complicated angelology and demonology of its own. There are good and evil angels. The latter are fallen, and take the forms of evil spirits and demons. They are usually visible only to spiritual eyes, but sometimes they materialize and can then be seen with physical eyes. They appear as witches, snakes and other reptiles, and are the same beings as pagans know under the name of obonsam, etc. for example in the syncretistic cult which recently flourished, Tigare, was really an impure spirit whose true name was Subusu. (The head of the Church provided this information orally). Concerning the good spirits, there are seven known 'Powerful angels who bear the Church in their arms' (from the Prophecies for 1957). Their names are: Michiel, Gabriel, Raphiel, Zaphiel, Zadkiel, Carmiel, and Harniel. Apart from these, there are seven Ministering angels who are sent to 'stay with the Church,' taking turns year by year. 'They are secret servants. Their names should not be mentioned in a mere conversation and whenever it is necessary to pronounce these names the act should be followed by prayer. These names should be "written with hand and be kept in your rooms" (bedrooms). Prayers should be said learning or mentioning the names aloud in public. These angels will do many kinds of services to you in healing, travelling and comforting the sufferer.' (Prophecies for 1957 Programme, p.12f.).

Church Government

The Supreme council and ruling body of the Church is the Jehunano Family. The word Jehunano is said to mean 'companions of Jehu' or 'followers of Jehu,' and the name referred originally to the group which moved out with the founder of the Church to the first Mazano. The council is perpetuated by appointing the sons of members who die, to succeed their fathers, provided, of course, that they are themselves members of the Church.[5] The Akaboha is President of the Council and exercises, in the Church, functions corresponding to those of a Bishop. All ministers, prophets and prophetesses are members, regardless of whether or not they were with the founder or are related to any of his companions. Apart from prophetesses, women can only come in as wives of members, not in their own right.

Eight to ten members of the Jehunano Family must always be present at Mazano. Those on duty in this way hold regular prayer meetings for short periods, five times each day, and must be available at all other times to make special intercessions in case of any need. They also deal with urgent emergency business referred to headquarters for decision from all parts of the Church. For this reason they may not engage in any business of their own, and may not even tend their own vegetable gardens, but are supported by members of the Church with gifts, both of money and in kind.[6]

Synod

The MDCC Synod or General Assembly (both terms are used) is officially known as the I'Odomey Conference. It is composed of all the clergy, with eight other members of the Jehunano Family, and one steward and one elder from each circuit. This annual conference, which was first held at Adwumaku Afransi on January 20th 1932, deals with all matters concerning the Church, spiritual as well as temporal. However, all major decisions are taken by the Jehunano Family alone. The clergy, apart from participating in I'Odomey, have a conference of their own called Zimadey,[7] which may submit requests and other matters directly to Jehunano for consideration.

Societies

'Societies' on the Methodist pattern, with sonorous names, abound within the Church. Some of these are: Ali-Sala, Disconsa Sett, Alishidani, Nahatim, Bewdney Lodge, Nathalomoa Band and Musama Scholars' Union.[8] Regular quarterly meetings, known as Seenim, are held in the provinces for spiritual revival, whereas 'camp' meetings may be organized at any time for special prayer help in divine healing.

The Ministry

The Ministry is in three sections, each subdivided into three grades as follows:

(a) The Clergy, of whom the most senior is called 'High Priest'; the others follow in descending order of seniority from grade 1 to grade 3. Promotion within the grades and from one to the next higher is said to be both by length of service and by efficiency. The clergy are ordained, administer the sacraments, bless marriages, and supervise the work of the catechists. Each is posted at the most important centre of his circuit, and carries out visitation within it.

(b) The catechists, likewise grouped into three grades, are in charge of the local branches or congregations. They hold the various meetings and services and, especially in the more out-of-the-way places, are very actively engaged in persuading people to send their sick to their church for healing. Otherwise, as is the case with the ministers also, their functions follow closely those of their opposite numbers in the historical Churches, excepting that they do not have to do with schools.⁹ They are all men and must be literate in Fanti.

The 'Prophetic' Ministry is carried out by men and women who are grouped into (a) full, (b) junior and (c) probational prophets and prophetesses, and their leader is known as the 'Senior Prophet.' They are the specialists in such activities (called 'spiritual'), as speaking in 'tongues,' invoking 'spirits,' detecting witches and other evil persons, exorcising devils, having and interpreting dreams and visions, predicting the future, foreseeing future misfortunes and prescribing measures to avert them and, more especially, discerning the 'spiritual' causes of illnesses. Those who do not hold this office in conjunction with preaching, especially the women, are mostly illiterate.

The Healing ministry. The healers are also in three grades according to the number and importance of the successes claimed for them. Those persistently failing to effect cures are relieved of their office, such lack of accomplishment being regarded as a sign that they never had the 'spirit,' or that he has abandoned them. Literacy is not required for healers.

It is possible and even common for one person to combine two, and in the case of men, all three of these ministries. The official workers must be either ordained or consecrated for their ministry in the Church. They are not paid fixed salaries, but receive a quarterly grant, varying in amount from time to time, when the Church's total income is shared at Mazano. This grant is said to average £21 per quarter for ministers, slightly less than this amount for prophets, and £15 per quarter for catechist. Prophetesses and female healers receive only token sums. The grant for Akaboha himself is said to be in the neighbourhood of £90 per quarter, some of it being regarded as an allowance for entertainment.

Although all the male agents are expected to devote their full time to the Church's business, nearly all of them do in fact engage in part time work of their own, mostly as farmers, or in the various trades which they had learnt before taking up church work, such as tailoring, brick-laying, carpentry, etc. wherever at all-possible, everyone engages in some vegetable gardening. The church administration raises no official objection so long as a man's work for the Church is proceeding satisfactorily. All the same, private business is viewed with disfavour.

The Akaboha thinks that, since the church work on the whole is progressing rapidly, agents ought to have enough on their hands to keep them fully occupied, and would do much better if they would give up these various sidelines. The church members support their workers in various ways, particularly by making and helping to maintain vegetable gardens for them. The result is that many of them are able to accumulate considerable amounts of money at headquarters as savings, through not drawing their grants when due.

Training

The training of the workers is on the in-service pattern, and is carried out mainly at Mazano. A training course for ordained and consecrated workers only, called the Finusifim, is held twice a year, and lasts from one to three weeks each time. Its objects are to inculcate a thorough knowledge of the special rites, and to promote skill in the accurate performance of the complicated ceremonial practised by the MDCC. Such an arrangement is all the more important since this ritual itself is in constant evolution, account being taken of new revelations as they are received. The elders of the Church, who assist the paid officers in the local groups upon a voluntary basis, are also given a course known as the Omisharong, at Mazano, twice a year, each course being of one week's duration. Leaders of congregational singing go to Mazano from time to time to learn new songs and new techniques of leading the singing.

Church Finance

The theory is tithing, but in fact people give as they fell inclined, the most generous offerings being made as thanksgiving for, or in expectation of, cures. In every chapel or meeting-place a collection-box is placed in front of the preacher's table, and worshippers drop their offerings into it as they enter the room. The men incline their heads as they do so, the women curtsy. On Sundays (in the smaller places after each meeting) the box is opened and the contents are counted and handed to the elder appointed as 'steward,' for safekeeping. One-fifth of the collections are retained for local expenses, and the rest is dispatched to Mazano for the central fund. The available figures of the Church's annual income are so few, and show such great variation from year to year that it is difficult to discern any trends or draw any other useful conclusions from them.[10] Besides, some of the figures appear to have been rounded up.

Sacred Places

The tomb of the first Akahoba and Founder of the Church, built prominently in the centre of Mazano, does not appear to play any part in the religious practices observed, but there are two other structures which do. These are the 'House of the Holy Well,' and the 'Holy Place.' The first contains a large water cistern, into which rainwater is collected from the roof of an adjacent house. This tank is fenced in and kept under lock and key. The water drawn from here is called 'holy water,' and is used for rubbing patients as part of the healing process as well as for baptism and certain special ceremonial ablutions. Outstations must always keep supplies on hand for official use. Some members go to Mazano or send there to fetch this water in bottles, and use it sparingly, for drinking only. It is believed that it both restores health after illness and maintains it.

The Holy Place, bearing this inscription, is a flat-roofed, oval-shaped cement house, standing by itself on slightly raised ground, in an enclosed courtyard. It is surmounted by a crown moulded in cement and a slab which bears its name. In front of the door, which is kept securely locked, is a man-size statue of an angel. A large wooden cross, painted white, stands before the entrance to the enclosure.

In this 'Holy Place,' also known as the 'Sanctum,' are to be found the Ark, the Book of the Holy Covenants, and the 'Holy See.' Here the final rites are carried out for the ordination of ministers and the consecration of prophets. The ordinand accompanies the Akaboha into the Holy Places; after certain ceremonies have been performed there, the Akaboha proceeds alone into the 'Holy of Holies' to pray on behalf of the ordinand and of the Church; the installation in office is completed when the two again emerge from the 'Holy Place,' the Akaboha holding the hand of the new minister or prophet. Apart from the Akaboha no one may enter the 'Holy of Holies' at any time.

In that place there is a spot at which the Akaboha may stand to pray at any hour of very special or urgent need, either of the Church or of the country as a whole. It was revealed to the Akaboha by an angel whom he saw in a vision standing at this spot that, if in any really pressing emergency he would stand there to pray, God would unfailingly hear, and send the aid of his Holy Spirit. It is this spot that is known in MDCC terminology as The Holy See, apparently also as the Mercy Seat.

The chapel at Mazano is, however, only a very modest structure, poorly furnished and kept. It is explained that no more money is being spent on it as plans are already far advanced to build a 'cathedral.' In fact a few quite imposing concrete pillars have already been erected, and in the meantime most services are being held under the large shed made of palm branches a few hundred yards away. It is pointed out that the standard MDCC chapel is the one at Agona Kwanyaku. Externally it is no different from the usual church building in Ghana. The internal arrangement combines the Methodist-type preacher's table (upon it a white cloth and a simple wooden cross, before it the collection-box) with a high-church altar against the wall in the rear, upon which a read curtain is hung. The altar holds a wooden frame for candles, and it is here that a candle-lighting ceremony and 'high mass' are held on Sunday whenever a priest is available. The holding of the 'high mass' ceremony is not permitted to any but advanced priests. No one may enter any MDCC place of worship wearing any sort of foot-gear.

Sacred Objects

The Ark is a box which contains the Ten commandments, the promises made by God to the MDCC through the first Akaboha, and the vows taken by the latter on behalf of the Church in respect of these promises, together with some of his prophecies, all written on parchment. The Ark, with this 'Book of the Holy Covenants' in it, may be carried round the town of Mazano in a holy procession at any time of national crisis, such as earthquakes, disease epidemics, or civic upheavals, whereupon God would avert extreme disaster.

Other objects may be added in the future. For example, the *Prophecies* for 1957 adumbrate the creation of a new 'Stone of Courtesy' as follows:

All the members should place a stone as a sign of your gratefulness that I the Lord have never lied to you before. This stone should be known as the Stone of Courtesy of God's truth to the MDC Church. It will be known in Fanti as NOKWAR BO (literally Stone of truth or faithfulness). This should be arranged to have this occasion during any high Anniversary when a greater number of the MDC Church members have assembled. I will instruct the Akaboha fully about this as to the time and place where this stone will be laid. The stone should be the size of about five times the fist of a man's hand. The Akaboha will anoint this stone and be covered by a wall of about two to three feet in length, breadth and height. Through this stone, I shall add more spiritual gifts to the Church. (pp. 13-14 of Special Programme of the 7th Peaceful Year Celebration at the New Mazano, Aug-Sep. 1957).

Sacred Dress

The ministers, prophets and catechists of this Church wear long white gowns buttoned in front, with blue, black, or purple girdles. For ceremonial occasions the higher clergy wear variously coloured copes and turbans in addition, whereas the Akaboha himself is resplendent in archiepiscopal vestments complete with mitre or biretta. For healing services the gown is red. Ordinary male members wear for divine service, as a rule, the plain white gown without buttons or girdle; women wear no gowns, but cover their heads (even if already covered by the handkerchief which is a part of women's ordinary dress) with a plain, i.e. unpatterned, cloth, red for healing and week-day services, white for Sundays and high occasions. As soon as 'ecclesiastical regalia' (the term in regular use for sacred apparel in this Church's literature) are donned, a member is presumed to have left the ordinary secular sphere and to have entered the realm of spiritual things;

he is expected, accordingly, to take on a serious attitude, to refrain from doing any unworthy act and from all loose or frivolous talk, and to concentrate his mind upon holy thoughts. The white gown is regarded as a sign of victory and the red as a reminder of the blood of Christ.

Religious Practice

MDCC is Anabaptist. Every new member must be baptized, whether he has previously received this sacrament or not, and regardless of which Church may have baptized him. The rite is performed in church by sprinkling with holy water and the laying on of hands. This is preceded by confession of sins, renunciation of the world with its lust, and an undertaking to abide by the Ten Commandments as well as the rules and regulations of the Church. At the first visit of the Akaboha after his baptism every new member receives a 'heavenly name,' by which he is officially known within the Church, though he retains his former names for all other purposes. The Akaboha claims that he goes to the naming ceremony without any preparation other than a spiritual one, but that after prayer he is able to read the heavenly name from the neophyte's own forehead.[11] This new name, often ponderous in sound, is greatly valued by the members.

Instruction then follows, mainly in the use of the 15-bead rosary, with the heavenly name of each bead, and its meaning and function;[12] in the Ten Commandments and the Lord's Prayer (when these are not already known); in certain forms of greetings in the heavenly tongue used by MDCC member among themselves, as well as responses said at church services in the same language, and in the MDCC version of the Apostles' Creed.

Infant baptism is also practiced, but is only administered to the children or wards of members, wherever possible in conjunction with the traditional Ghanaian custom of 'out-dooring.'

From the time of his baptism onward, every member is under obligation to wear around his neck at all times, over or under his clothing, a small wooden crucifix on a thin metal chain. They are procurable from Mazano, where they are made.

Several fasts are held in this Church, and great importance is attached to them. The 'ordinary' fast is on every Friday, from waking up until 6 o'clock pm. During this fast only water and the chewing of cola are allowed. The fast is obligatory for all members excepting expectant mothers, the sick, and those advanced in age. The 'special' fast for ordinary members involves abstention from fish and meat of all kinds, as well as salt, pepper, or any other kind of condiment, for a period of three days. Milk and unsweetened pap[13] are allowed in moderate quantities only.

The clergy hold fasts with complete self-denial of all foods, as prescribed from time to time by the Akaboha. These fasts may be for three or seven days, but never exceed seven days at a time. It is said that during the dry months from December to March, fasting is particularly difficult because of excessive heat and thirst; in very hard years, therefore, the circuit superintendent, with the Akaboha's permission, may grant dispensation in respect of oranges and bananas, but no other food may be allowed. There is an obligatory fast for all clergy during the three days immediately preceding the beginning of the great annual meeting and festival, the 'Peaceful Year Celebration.'

Members holding any kind of fast must also refrain absolutely from sexual intercourse and from indulging in any indecent joking or conversation; rather they should keep their minds steadfastly upon good and hold thoughts alone.

'System' Prayer

This is usually combined with fasting and consists in the performance of certain rituals prescribed ad hoc to meet specific situations of impending danger or suffering (called 'travail'). These threats are perceived spiritually. To advert them, the 'system' might require a member to recite a certain prayer at certain places so many times a day while holding a palm branch in the right hand, or dressed completely in white, or standing before three lighted candles, etc., etc. A 'system' prayer with fasting is more effective than ordinary prayers because it is tailored to the requirements of the particular evil that is to be avoided. It can only be prescribed by the Akaboha. It is found necessary from time to time both for individuals and for the whole Church.

During *the preparation for 'The Peaceful Year,'* which is the great annual festival of the connection, a 'Stool Celebration Day' is kept. On at least one such occasion in the past, a sheep was slaughtered and burnt as sacrifice. (The slaughtering of sheep is, of course, an essential part of Akan customary stool rites). This practice has, however, been discontinued, and the present usage is for the sheep to be treated in a way reminiscent of Old Testament procedure at the Feast of Atonement.

In a service of prayer and supplication the sheep is taken and 'presented before God' with the request that any harm that might be 'in the air' and about to descend upon the people during the festival should come instead upon the sheep. The animal is then tied to a tree with a rope throughout the duration of the festival. It is believed that if indeed there were some harm coming to the people, the sheep would die. In such a case, the Jehunano Family would at once proclaim a stringent fast, and special prayer sessions, with 'systems,' would be held to implore God's mercy. If the sheep does not die by itself, it is slaughtered and burnt as burnt-offering of thanksgiving on the first Saturday in August, which is the end of the preparation. A successful and happy 'Peaceful Year' celebration is thus assured, nobody need have any more anxieties on this score.

It is reported that in 1956 the sheep did die, and there was a lorry accident involving people travelling to the festival. It was said that if there had not been this warning and the measures which because of it could be taken to avert the disaster, the death-toll would have been catastrophic. In fact, although the accident was of a very serious nature, all in the lorry escaped with no more than slight bruises and other equally minor injuries.

The *service of worship* includes evangelistic preaching of a very pronounced revivalist character, and the singing of many African chants with strongly marked rhythm. The MDCC has developed a great wealth of Fanti lyric music with words on the usual themes of evangelistic-revivalist preaching. During the course of a sermon the trained songster on duty (sometimes also any other member of the congregation feeling so moved) would suddenly and dramatically intone an appropriate song and lead the rest in singing it for a while, before the preaching is resumed, quite in the fashion of the telling of African folklore. This interruption occurs several times during the services, and the piercing words and melodies, as well as the rhythmic swaying-sometimes even dancing-of the congregation to the music, greatly heightens the general effect of the service, and appears to afford much satisfaction to many of the worshippers. There are sometimes also other demonstrations of irrepressible feeling, such as ejaculations, ecstatic shrieks, and violent rocking almost to the point of exhaustion. The men and women chosen and trained to be 'songsters' all have powerful voices and considerable emotional and dramatic address, and hardly ever fail completely to produce some at least of the effects described.

In certain types of services, African drumming may be brought into play to assist the music, and then the dancing becomes more general and less restrained. This is particularly the case with services in which a healing session is combined with the worship. It is reported that at first the founder of the Church was inclined to frown upon drumming and dancing in connection with worship. It is reported that at the first the founder of the Church was inclined to frown upon drumming and dancing in connection with worship, but on one occasion, after he had rebuked his followers on this points, he had a vision and saw angels likewise his followers on this point, he had a vision and saw angels likewise disporting themselves. He thereby got to know that these activities were fully permitted in the service of God, and told his people so. However, those who try to go over to nonreligious dancing (African or Western style) are restrained, and ballroom dancing of partners of opposite sexes is strictly prohibited upon pain of exclusion from the Church.

Men and women sit separately at chapel, and do not mix for any church activities.

'High Mass' and the ceremony of lighting the candles have been mentioned. The sacrament of *Holy Communion* is administered once every three months and also at Easter and during the 'Peaceful Year Celebration.' The whole of the previous day must be spent in self-preparation. All outstanding disputes must have been settled, there is confession of sins, and a general cleaning of one's house, clothes, and other personal effects. There may be no sexual intercourse. At midnight the minister alone takes the elements to the chapel, places them upon the communion table and blesses them. There they remain until the service of celebration begins, usually soon after 4 o'clock a.m. If the congregation is large, the service begins earlier still, as it is timed to come to an end just before dawn. The administration of communion follows the Methodist rite, with an obligatory reading of John 6. 47-58.

Taboos

The MDCC enjoins total abstinence from all alcoholic drinks as well as from the use of tobacco in any form. The food taboos are pork, monkeys (because they have faces, hands, and feet like men), bush rats, blood and any dead animal or fowl, i.e. one not expressly slaughtered for eating. Formerly there were special regulations excluding women from participation in services of worship and all other public functions during their monthly period; at present, although such regulations have been abandoned or greatly relax, the women voluntarily keep themselves apart during this time 'in order to increase their own purity.'[14] In fact, practically all the women in this Church continue to observe the old regulations.[1]

Divine Healing

At an evening prayer meeting of this Church in a small provincial town, the catechist began his address as follows: 'We are all in this Church because we have found healing here. But for this Church the great majority of us here assembled would not be alive today. That is the reason why we are here: is that not so?' To that question came from the congregation as answer, a unanimous and most decided 'Yes!'

Healing is undoubtedly far and away the most important activity of the Church. Although the Akaboha claims member who have joined for reasons other than an effected or expected cure, such must be very few indeed.

MDCC members are not allowed the use of any drugs whatsoever, and may be treated in the hospital only for accidents involving some abrupt break of a bodily organ. It is not permitted for them to consult either Western-trained doctors or African herbalists, whereas resort to a medicine man, or to magical healing or any kind, is regarded as one of the most serious offences that can be committed, and is punishable by prompt expulsion from the Church. Members may visit doctors only when a medical certificate is required of them for obtaining employment or some official document or other similar purpose.

In his history of the early days of the Church, the founder has a chapter devoted to the elaboration of his position on this point. He expresses surprise that there are Christians who do not seem to know that God is the only true Healer of all men's diseases. This elementary knowledge of God is accessible even to pagan witchdoctors, because when they express hope for a cure, they invariably say: '...if it be the will of God.' In Ex. 15. 26[16] God plainly describes himself as the healer of all man's diseases. Furthermore, God's healing proceeds from his power and does not depend upon leaves, herbs and roots. When in Mark 16. 15-18[17] Jesus promised supernatural powers to his disciples including the power of healing diseases, he said that the source of this power would be his name, not that it was in the virtues of plants. It is therefore surprising to find Christians making the point that, since God created the plants, he means men to use them as medicine. If that were so, it should be ministers and other workers of God who should dispense these medicines, but that is not the case. In the story in Matt. 17, 14-21 it is clear that the cause of the disciples' failure to heal was lack of faith. The present Akaboha adds that, since every illness has a spiritual cause, it should be dealt with 'spiritually.'

The central healing establishment, called after the Queenmother 'Nathalomoa Camp,' is the most important of all the buildings at Mazano. The premises consist of a very spacious compound with three major buildings. The main one is a large meeting hall furnished with benches and a leader's table. At one end of it is a decorated porch upon which stands the statue of an angel; at the other end are cubicles for the private treatment of special cases. On the other side of the compound is a house with eight rooms all in a row for the accommodation of patients. The third building contains a restroom for the attendants and an enquiry office.

Patients prepare themselves for the healing service by holding the prescribed fast and, upon the day of the service, ceremonially washing themselves. While repeating a set prayer for this purpose,[18] they must wash meticulously all the orifices of their body, and their armpits.

A service of worship and exhortation usually precedes the healing activities. It is called *Sunsumfie Asore* or service for the invocation of the spirit. There are usually three rounds of prayers, during which anyone feeling so moved may present his or her petition aloud. The rest of the worshippers join in by interjecting an 'Amen' after each definite petition with which they would identify themselves, and by showing various other signs of lively participation. Each round of prayers is brought to an end by the stroke of a bell, whereupon there is some singing of appropriate Fanti lyrics. The prayers are concluded by the leader who, beginning rather quietly and with a calm voice, works himself up by degrees to such a pitch of piercing eloquence and the most intensely passionate appeal, that the whole atmosphere becomes emotionally highly charged. People, already on their knees, throw out their arms and lean backwards, looking up with the most beatific facial expressions; others prostrate and beat upon the ground; still others sigh and sob as they turn their bodies constantly to the right and to the left; many weep aloud, and there are various other expressions of self-abasement, devotion and importunity.

At this point the songsters and drummers strike up, and soon there is general dancing or swaying to songs pleading for mercy and for healing. The consecrated healers and their auxiliaries put on their red copes and range themselves in a semi-circle before the Chief Healer. He blesses the large bottles of olive oil standing on the table, pours some saucers. He than dips his fingers into the oil and, going round the semi-circle, holds and rubs both forearms and hands of each healer and auxiliary healer, pronouncing words about Christ having given his followers power to heal, and a prayer that the healers may have that power. He then hands the saucers to them, and they go out among the patients.[19]

Each patient coming forward is asked what his ailment is; he is then rubbed with the oil very thoroughly on the part of the body in question, the healer praying the while that the patient's sins may be forgiven and that God himself would restore him to health. The singing and drumming continues the whole time, and so do the demonstrations of exigence and solicitude. When the people are about to weary, the leader calls to order and offers a concluding prayer in which he thanks God for all who have found healing.

A session then follows, almost oddly calm in comparison with what has gone on before. Very quietly people are asked to come forward and 'witness' to any change for the better in their condition, which they may have experienced during the healing exercises. Often there would be some to say that they felt a sudden pull, or jerk; or that something had snapped within them; or that they had had a sensation of cold (or warm) currently running through their body from head to toe (or in the contrary direction); and all would express confidence that this signified the sure beginning of their cure. Sometimes this confidence is so great that the patient feels that he is already completely cured, and says so with great joy and thankfulness to God. Someone in the audience would shout 'Halleluia!' or 'Praise be!' or some such piously jubilant exclamation, whereupon a songster would break into some appropriate lyric, in which all present would join heartily to sing. But after a while there would be calm and silence once more, so that the next witness may be heard.

Almost any kind of illness and disease is brought for healing. Some sort of record of the cases is kept, but its object being really only to register their numbers, the descriptions of the ailments are extremely vague. Such entries as 'the whole body,' 'head,' 'backside,' 'cough,' etc., abound. Since, however, in the nature of the circumstances there cannot be any kind of competent diagnosis, the young and inexperienced scribe usually in charge of the record can only put down what the patients say they are suffering from.

In March 1958 there were as many as eight mental patients at the Nathalomoa Camp at Mazano, all so violent that they had to be chained in their rooms. The treatment of such cases in undertaken separately from that of other ailments. It proceeds in private, and a lot of time is given to each individual patient. Apart from the application of 'holy water' and consecrated oil, exorcism is employed as well as a procedure similar to hypnotic suggestion, accompanied with incessant prayer by the other assisting officials present.

One of the troubles quite frequently brought for cure is involuntary witchcraft. This generally afflicts women, but a few men suffer from it as well. The complaint is that, by some means known or unknown to them, and in any case without their own wish, they have had an accession of the witch's supernatural power to harm others, and they are most anxious to be rid of it.[20] The Akaboha says that formerly such cases were considered as greatly embarrassing to the persons concerned (since others thereafter avoided them as much possible), and so they were treated privately and mostly at night. Now, however, people do not seem any more to mind being treated publicly and in open daylight. Their healing involves a lot of exorcism

At the outstations manned by priests or healers there is a divine healing session every Friday throughout the year (excepting Good Friday and the Fridays of the Festival) at the 'Camp,' beginning about 9.30 am and going on till about 4 pm. It is preceded by an early morning service at 5.30 on the theme of the precious blood of Christ; sometimes, especially when particularly difficult or important cases are to be treated, there is a still earlier service at midnight from Thursday to Friday.

The Akaboha once made the interesting remark that it was extremely difficult to heal pagans because they did not understand what faith was.

The 'Casting of Lots'

In the custom, peculiar to this Church, which is known by this name, the prophet lays his hand on the head of each of those members who come forward for this purpose, and 'describes (his or her) spiritual condition.' This consists in telling whether or not the spirit concerned is in a healthy condition and a happy mood, or whether it is being assailed, or is about to be assailed by some spirit of evil or misfortune. In the latter case the precautions necessary for the safety of the person concerned, are prescribed. Also, a person's future may be foretold. The directions regarding the precautionary measures to be taken are given in terms both explicit and precise, so that no one can be in any doubt as to what he is required to do, but the predictions are of a general character, similar to that of the prophecies published annually. They are said to be greatly valued by the members of the Church.

Marriage, and Family Regulation

The MDCC is trying to practise what may be called controlled polygamy. It appears to be assumed that polygamy is the form of marriage willed by God. The relevant Church rule simply says: 'Everybody is to marry according to God's will.' (This has now been stated more explicitly, thus: 'We believe that [as an African Church] polygamy is not moral sin.' See No. 18 in Appendix B 1.) However, for each such marriage to be recognized within the Church, it should have been officially blessed, and for the ceremony of blessing to take place, it is necessary to obtain permission from Jehunano itself. When an application for such permission is receive, the authorities take care to inform themselves thoroughly, through their agents, of all the circumstances of the matter before they decide whether or not 'it is necessary and fitting' that the petitioners should marry. It is said that where the prospective bridegroom is already married and has proved unable or reluctant to care for his wife or wives adequately, or where he intends to marry a woman promised in marriage to some other member of the church, or where the circumstances are such that some sort of trouble resulting from the union may be anticipated, permission is refused. Again, where the intending bridegroom already has several wives, the authorities try to dissuade him from taking more.21

The decision, however, is not based upon such merely practical or prudential considerations only, for a 'spiritual consultation' is also held on behalf of the intending partners. It is stated that is would usually be found that the spirits of the parties whose union Jehunano in its wisdom has disapproved, are really incompatible; or that in the spiritual realm they are threatened with some disaster if they should pursue their purpose.

In view of this possibility of knowing in advance about the fate of a marriage, many people (including even non-members of the Church, it is reported), when they intend to marry, first write to Mazano for spiritual consultation, to find out what chances of success the marriage stands before embarking upon it. At times two or three names of prospective spouses are submitted for choice. Some have been known to desist when the oracle was unfavourable.[22]

A rule of the Church says that every wife shall bow before her husband (and, in fact, any other man) when speaking or offering something to him or receiving anything from him. A wife shall call her husband 'Papa,' which the Queenmother explains by giving the reason that, since the husband has assumed the duties and responsibilities towards his wife which her father formerly discharged, he has, in fact, become his wife's 'father,' and should be so recognized.

No *divorce* of persons married in the MDCC is allowed for any cause whatsoever. Those who do so divorce automatically exclude themselves from continued membership of the Church.

Marriage counselling is very actively pursued in this Church. Apart from the local leader's efforts to help individual families in their homes, at least once a month in every church a 'marriage meeting' is held, devoted entirely to discussions of marriage and of family life. During the annual festival one of the high occasions is the 'Marriage meeting,' which is addressed by prominent men and women specially invited to come and give their good advice on these matters. Those within the Church who do this counselling are, however, not specifically trained for this purpose, and carry on this aspect of the work only from their own common sense and experience of life.

The MDCC is also setting its hand to the rectification or the amelioration of some African customs which have been causing difficulties among families. It encourages 'son inheritance' and requires all fathers at least to share responsibility for the upbringing of all their children.[23] The long observance of Fanti widowhood rites has been well known as a source of great hardship for the women concerned. The MDCC has ruled that their widows shall observe these customs only for 6-12 weeks (instead of one year and longer). Even so it is only a very modified form of the usages which are allowed to be practised; all purely heathen parts of them, such as shaving the head completely and bathing in the sea at dead of night, being strictly forbidden.

The same effort to relieve the burden of traditional custom may be traced in the burial and funeral practices adopted by the MDCC. During the watchnight for a deceased member, only tea, coffee or coconut milk may be served as refreshments and no alcohol, locally brewed or imported, is allowed. All the costs of a deceased member's funeral are borne by the fellow-members who, in order to control spending, take things in hand themselves. The Church, however, does not try to interfere with local custom in regard to the disposal of a deceased member's estate, as it does not wish to become involved in law-suit.

The MDCC administers extreme unction to its dying members; in accordance with the Old Testament regulations, it does not permit the carrying of a corpse into a place of worship. The coffin may, however, be brought as far as the church door from where, after biblical passages have been recited and prayers said over it, it is taken to the cemetery for burial according to the Methodist rite.

[3]

This is the largest and most highly organized of the indigenous 'spiritual churches' in Ghana. Its headquarters, New Mazano, is situated upon land purchased by the Church for the sum of nearly £1,000, which estate is large enough to hold a fair-sized village. The settlement presents a quite pleasant aspect as it is approached from a commemorative pillar placed in the middle of its only motor road, on the boundary with the adjacent village of Gomoa-Eshiem, Agona Swedru district. From this point the land inclines gently downwards towards the marketplace, where it begins to rise again. The houses are disposed on either hand of a very broad central thoroughfare leading to the marketplace, obviously intended by the layout to be the centre of the town. In the middle of the market-place stands prominently the tomb of the founder of the MDCC, planted with lush canna flowers and fenced in by an ornate decorative cement wall. On the rising beyond the market-place are situated the chapel, the house of the 'Holy Well,' the 'Holy Place,' the general offices of the Church administration, the dwelling-houses of some leading Jehunano Family members and of the Akatitibi; while a little to the right stands in dignified aloofness and pleasing simplicity, the bungalow-type official residence of the head of the Church.

Apart from a number of those who are in Mazano temporarily for healing, all the inhabitants are staunch members of the Church. I was informed that many members, who have to live elsewhere for their work, maintain at Mazano a pied-a-terre of some sort, so that they can go and stay there whenever they are free to do so. Besides, the community as a whole has provided extensive accommodation for the housing of patients and other visitors, particularly the participants in the various church conferences and the annual great festival. I was further told that many prominent members of the Church hoped to spend the last years of their lives at Mazano.

This Church has drawn on various sources to establish a pattern all its own. The organization of the field into 'circuits,' the method of raising money and its oversight by 'stewards,' the type and manner of preaching adopted, substantial sections of the prayer-book and other features are plainly Methodist, whereas the 'High Mass' and candles, the vestments and the ceremonial on high occasions are admittedly taken from the Anglo-Catholic tradition. With these are combined, particularly from the common life as apart from worship and administration, a number of elements from Akan chieftaincy and traditional African clan life. In Yorke's History (still in MS) as well as in some of the literature produced for the annual festival, the head of the Church is referred to as Omanhene or 'Paramount Chief,' sometimes also as 'King'; while his mother, officially known as the Akatitibi, is styled queenmother. A paragraph in the printed programme for the 1951 celebration, entitled Chieftaincy in the Kingdom of the MDC Church, assigns to individuals and local branches the various positions of responsibility and of honour in the Akan political hierarchy. The Akaboha II explained to me that their Abura circuit, being the 'first-born,' held the title Abatan; other circuits held the positions of Akan martial dispositions indicated, as follows: Agona-Adonten; Adwumako-Nifa; Ewutu-Benkum; New Juaben and Accra-Kyidom; Breman-Twafo.

In his 'Seventh Year Speech 1948-1955,' as he lists the rapid improvements which had taken place during his term of office, he writes: 'During my reign ... I have raised the standard of chieftaincy in the MDC Church.'

The Church sometimes 'sits as a State,' when these various functionaries take up their positions, and court is held in Akan fashion to hear and determine non-spiritual causes arising within the Church. This is called the Piodama meeting. It appears to be a standing order (since it is repeated in practically all available anniversary programmes) that African dress should be worn for the Piodama meeting.

This use of the African heritage in building up the structure of the Church is not surprising, for in his booklet the founder shows himself to have been a typical ardent Gold Coast nationalist of a generation ago. He was concerned to reassert the value of Africa institutions and customs in the face of what he considered to be an all-too indiscriminate rejection of them in favour of European ways. This is attested, among other things, by his life-membership of the Aborigines' Rights Protection Society, a political and cultural association of Gold Coast patriots centring in Cape Coast, and of long standing, whose main object is stated in its name.

Not only did the founder himself maintain these interests till his death, but he also passed them on to his successors, with the result that the MDCC is the 'spiritual church' with the most pronounced interest in customary practices and national politics in Ghana today. The present Akaboha relates how his father, having predicted that independence would eventually come to the country, but not through the Aborigines' Rights Protection Society, was deluged with enquires from his followers at the time when Dr. Kwame Nkrumah first started to canvass for support. People wanted know whether the latter was the person whom the prophecy had envisaged, and even now, at the time of general elections, some members would write in for spiritual consultation, in order to be advised how to cast their votes in the best interests of the country. After the political disturbances of 1948, the founder himself welcomed Dr. Kwame Nkrumah to Mazano for purification from his arrest and brief deportation; his successor invited the Prime Minister for blessing at the 'Peaceful Year' anniversary celebration in 1951 and 1953.[24]

There appears to be a definite intention to make of the members of this church a distinctive community within the larger society. Like all the other sects, the MDCC encourages its members to look upon one another as brothers and sisters, and so to address one another; but at Mazano, and to a lesser extent at the sub-stations also, other special efforts are undertaken to emphasize this point of belonging to a common family. Considerable mutual aid is practised, in goods and money as well as in services, and there is much sharing in one another's personal and family occasions and affairs, such as the outdooring of babies, engagements, marriages and the various customary arrangement therefore, other celebrations, serious court cases, sickness, bereavement, etc. of course, as already noted, the funeral of a deceased member is the responsibility of the whole Church, not of his family alone.

This inculcation of sense of belonging within a very special brotherhood is greatly strengthened by the use of a peculiar language. While this is not sufficiently extensive for all the purposes of ordinary communication, greetings and many other short phrases that frequently recur in conversation are expressed in this special language.[25] The common belief among member is that these words and phrases are from a heavenly language revealed to their founding prophet by angels. Together with the strange and impressive-sounding new name that each neophyte receives, this language creates an aura of mystery and 'spirituality' which is fascinating to members, and help not a little in furthering the cause. The various outward observances practised, such as the wearing of the little crucifix around the neck (frankly displayed by most, but hidden by some under their clothing), the rosary prayers publicly performed, the frequent local meetings for all sorts of purposes (usually conducted like a family meeting), the occasional pilgrimages to Mazano by individuals and small groups, etc, likewise serve the same purpose. By these means the MDCC both effectively maintains a very real uniting bond within its own membership, and consciously marks itself off from other fellow-citizens as 'a people part.'

At a time when the traditional bonds of family and kinship ties are rapidly disintegrating, and the mutual obligations previously recognized by blood relations are being repudiated, with the result that, for the first time (at least in Ghana), some Africans are finding themselves without dependable 'family' even in their own hometowns, the significance of this opportunity of accession to a new group capable of replacing the old cannot be exaggerated.

Some of the customs of the MDCC are strongly reminiscent of practices of the Yehwe Cult, a totally pagan secret society cult which is widespread in the Ewe country but practically unknown among the Akans. Some of the common (or very similar) practices are: 1. The adoption of a new name by the neophyte; 2. The use of a peculiar language; 3. The teaching to women novices of unquestioning obedience and humility towards the men set over them; and 4. The prohibition of the use of pepper and salt at certain times for ritual reasons.[26]

The priesthood of each head of a household, which is a feature of ancient African religion, seems to be suggested in the MDCC custom of Kanedua. This word means a lamp post, and the custom connected with in consists in the householder fixing one in the middle of his compound, and gathering all the inmates around a lighted lamp placed upon it for certain prescribed ceremonies and prayers before retiring night. I was informed, however, that ever fewer people were daring to set it up because once a Kanedua is installed, the custom must be regularly and meticulously performed, unless it is physically impossible to do so; and that, whereas great benefits resulted from a strict observance of the rites, neglect was sure to bring baneful consequences. The customs is now generally retained only as the conclusion of public evening prayer. At the end of the final hymn, a bell is rung, upon which the women file out; the bill is rung a second time, and the men follow, likewise in single line. The bell goes a third time, and the leader of the service takes out the main light which has been used for the meeting (usually a bright, pressure hurricane-lamp) and sets it on the lamp post about five feet high, fixed in front of the main entrance of the meeting-place. All assemble in a wide circle around the light, with heads bowed, and maintain silence for a while. Then the leader repeats certain set prayers, after each of which the men bow and the women curtsy. Then he says: 'Bahadum sakamo Obeko'; the people reply: 'Yam busudu moko ta, and disban.'[27]

A regular feature of the MDCC yearly almanac is the column on the 'Events of the Year, as prophesied by the Prophet M. M. Jehu-Appiah,

Akaboha II.' A sample of these prophecies is given in Appendix B. Substantially the same things are said the year in question in the programme printed for the anniversary celebration, but here a more personal note is adopted, and some additional revelations are made. God speaks intimately and in the first person to his people of the MDCC, his address being punctuated with familiar devices of Akan rhetoric, e.g. 'Moate?' ('Do you hear?') or 'Anaa?' ('Is that not so?')[28] In their form and content, these prophecies bear striking resemblance to the 'Messages' delivered by Father Divine of the USA in such of his publications as The New Day.

NOTES

[1] On one of my visits to Mazano I was given some of this liquid. It smelt like some cosmetic scent and had the consistency and taste of glycerine.

[2] Other available figures are as follows: for 1948, '49, '51, '54, and '56: 5,540, 6,170, 8,016, 8,280, and 14,000 respectively. Two different figures are given for 1955, i.e. 11,000 at p. 11 and 12,980 at p. 19 of the Fifth Peaceful Year Celebration programme. The figures point to steady and substantial increase. The 1959 Almanac gives the following statistic: number of pastors-30; number of catechists and healers - 94; number of stations - 90; number of sub-stations- 101; total membership - 19,800; total patients received - 4,716; total patients healed - 4,209; lapses - 398; deaths - 109.

[3] Also called 'supervising priest.' The terms 'minister' and 'priest' are used interchangeably in the MDCC.

[4] 1954 Peaceful Year Celebration Programme, p.14: 'We strongly detest superstitution, idolatry, occultism, fetishism, astrology, spiritualism, psychic science, etc.' In my interviews with him the Akaboha reiterated this point several times. When I suggested that some of his foreign correspondents (e.g., the 'Spiritual Discarnate Director of Harmonia College' of St. Petersburg, Florida, USA) might well be looked upon as occultists and that in fact some of their own practices might come under this classification, he said that this could not be the case, and proceeded to draw a distinction between 'spiritualist' and 'occultist' to the general effect that the latter implied sorcery and the use of evil spirits for nefarious ends. The matter remains difficult, however, since 'spiritualism' is itself in the above list of condemn practices. In point of fact, all the groups discussed in the present study, including the MDCC, describe themselves as 'spiritual churches.'

[5] This is an illustration of the effort by this Church to substitute 'son inheritance' for 'nephew inheritance.'

[6] I understand that these are on the whole inadequate, and that the Jehunano members have to depend largely on private income or on the labours of the members of their households. When I asked a MDCC local minister whether he would prefer headquarters service, he very vigorously expressed the hope that he would never be called upon to make that 'sacrifice.'

[7] Although all members know what these words stand for, their literal meaning is unattainable, as they are 'heavenly words' revealed. The Seenim meetings are an occasion for recruiting new members to the group. It was claimed that at a Seenim held at Larteh in Akwapim in March 1958, 74 sick were instantaneously healed, including 9 persons suffering from paralysis in the legs, who were able to hand in their walking sticks and crutches to be burnt; whereupon 50 new members joined the Church.

[8] See 1951 programme for Peaceful Year Celebration, last page, for a list of societies.

[9] The MDCC is not an educational unit, its sole school being the local Primary at Mazano.
[10] The available figures are as follows:

For the year:	1949	1951	1954	1955
Collected:	£790/5/6d;	£219/-/-d;	£4,121/7/4d;	£1,455/6/6d
Spent:	£700/15/11 ½d;	£179/-/-d;	£4,086/4/1 ½ d;	(not given)

I encountered some difficulty in eliciting information on the subject of the Church's finances, and what I got did not amount to much. Whereas on other points information was readily and gladly given, on this one there was an odd and striking reticence. For instance, to my question, whether all the workers, particularly the healers, turned in the patients' thanksgiving offerings to be paid into the central fund, I never got a clear answer. I visited a MDCC local priest in the company of Dr. Parsons of Hartford Seminary (USA). While he was chatting with the priest in English, the latter's wife, sitting a few yards away, was having the conversation translated into the vernacular for her by a grown-up daughter. When the woman heard her husband was telling Dr. Parsons that financial matters in the Church were running smoothly and that, while not having too much they had enough and were all happy, she exclaimed: 'O Papa has fallen! He is telling lies this early morning! If what you are saying were true, what is the source of all our many troubles?' Then she rose up and left.

[11] A country priest told me that a necessary condition is for the neophyte to hold the 'special fast.'

[12] The MDCC rosary is in five sections, in each of which the subject matter for prayer and meditation is as follows: 1. In the name of the Father, and of the Son and of the Holy Ghost, Amen; 2. Confession of sins; 3. The Ten Commandments, with a prayer to be able to keep them; 4. The Apostles' Creed (MDCC version). It has to be said three times over, each time ending with a prayer for the support of the Holy Spirit in holding firmly to this faith until the end; and 5. The Lord's Prayer, ending with a benediction called 'Blessing unto everlasting.' The Rosary prayer is known in MDCC terminology as Inaabi. It is to be said upon rising from bed, at noon, at nightfall, and when going to sleep. Those who have 'holy water' and drink of it at 6 a.m., must be careful to perform the Inaabi before they do so.

[13] 'Pap' is a light porridge made from Indian corn meal.

[14] Among practically all the tribes of Ghana in the old days the women, during their monthly period, had to live and sleep outside the house. Although this custom has largely fallen into disuse, some people still practise it.

[15] I was told this by a rural priest who maintained that the custom was required by the Church and who was thereupon informed by me that the Akaboha himself had said this was not the case.

[16] 'Saying, "If you will diligently hearken to the voice of the LORD your God, and do that which is right in his eyes, and give heed to his commandments and keep all his statues, I will put none of the diseases upon you which I put upon the Egyptians; for I am the LORD your healer."'

[17] And he said to them, "Go into all the world and preach the gospel to the whole creation. He who believes and is baptized will be saved; but he who does not believe will be condemned. And these signs will accompany those who believe: in my name they will cast out demons; they will speak in new tongues; they will pick up serpents, and if they drink any deadly thing, it will not hurt them; they will lay their hands on the sick; and they will recover."

[18] See Appendix B (3).

[19] Olive oil and 'holy water' may be used separately or together. When both are used, the patient is first rubbed with the water and then with the oil. Olive oil not obtained from Mazano must be sent there for blessing before it is used.

[20] An educated young woman who once requested a clergyman's help in ridding herself of involuntary witchcraft, when asked how she knew that she had such a power, said that twice she had had a presentiment of an event which came to pass, and once in a rage she had said to

someone who had angered her that God would repay him, and he had afterwards suffered a misfortune.

21 The Akaboha said that the ultimate aim was to allow ordinary members to have no more than three, and the clergy only up to two, wives. However, when I repeated this to a country priest, he seemed both surprised and amused and asked me, laughing: 'Is that what he said, really?'

22 In the Ewe country, a belief exists that every person has an ideal married partner in mawu-fe, i.e. God's world or heaven. If such a couple in fact meet and marry on earth, their married life is both successful and happy. Conversely, unsuccessful marriages are due to the fact that the wrong partners came together. Oracles are often consulted to find out whether people who intend to marry (especially when it is for the first time) are each other's partners in mawu-fe.

23 Among matrilineal descent groups such as the Gomoa and the Fanti, this is regarded as the responsibility of the maternal uncle.

24 This must not, however, be understood to imply any disloyalty to the previous regime. The anniversary programmes often end with the words: 'God save the King.'

25 For illustration, instead of the word 'Agoo' which a visitor uses to announce himself when he enters another's house, to which the reply is 'Amee,' the MDCC people say among themselves: 'Owula ka musaka?' to which the reply is 'Ali ibuka musuka,' if permission is granted to the caller to enter, and 'Monsi buka,' when he is required to wait outside a little.

26 J.Spieth, Die Religion der Eweer in Sud-Togo (Dieterich Verlag, Leipzig, 1911) pp. 172f.

27 This said to mean: (From the priest), 'May God be with you this night.' (From the people) 'May he be with you also superabundantly!'

28 As an illustration: 'Travail: And why do you require from me some system to prevent travails? Have I brought such curse upon you? Or has Satan conquered you in this way? I have been your midwife for a long time since I founded the MDC Church and through you I have saved the lives of many sufferers in this way. Not so? Why do you not appreciate my help and blessing? Prayer or system against travail should be an individual case and not a general one. You hear?' (1957 Programme, p. 13).

Prof. Baëta in his hood

CHAPTER FOUR

Memeneda Gyidifo (The Saviour Church)

[1]

THE English name of this body is hardly ever used, not being even known, except to a few. This is a very rural society in the sense that few, if any, large-town dwellers are members, and it is popularly called by its Ghanaian name of Memeneda Gyidifo, literally meaning 'Saturday Believers.' Its headquarters is at Osiem in the Tafo-Akim district of the Eastern Region of Ghana (Postal address P O Box 8), where it has its only substantial chapel building. This is a fairly solid structure measuring some 45 feet by about 20 feet, having a foundation of natural stones and cement, a cemented floor, thick, well-built mud walls and a roof of iron sheets. It is plainly furnished with simple benches and an ordinary leader's table.

The group claims a present membership of nearly 7,000. (The figure for 1954 was 3,421; no others are available). There is a fairly well-kept list of the local branches, which number 83, and are grouped into 11 'circuits,' each circuit being under a 'pastor.' A study of this list reveals that, with two exceptions, Tafo and Wenchi, and perhaps Osiem itself, all the places named are quite small villages.

The founder of this body was one Samuel Brako, a native of Osiem. He was a staunch Methodist, and for some time functioned as one of the Church's colporteurs, distributing vernacular Christian literature in the out-of-the-way rural areas. At some time about 1924 he began receiving messages from God in dreams. In particular God revealed to him that the day that he himself had set aside for rest and worship was Saturday, and not Sunday. 'Why,' God had asked, 'will my people not do as I say?' This disobedience, it was disclosed to him, was the real cause of the Church's failure to make progress in its efforts to stop adultery and drunkenness. He received this revelation repeatedly over a period, and finally God commanded him to go out and correct this grievous error that was being committed by churches.

Early one morning in that same year he started to preach about these things. People were at first surprised to see him doing so, and were curious to learn what he had to say; but soon they turned to mocking him. The Church authorities would not pay any heed to the messages he had for them from God. But he fearlessly continued his work, depending upon God alone, and preached that the Ten Commandments should be strictly observed, particularly that the Sabbath should be kept on Saturday; that there should be no irregular sexual relations or drinking of intoxicating liquors of any kind, and no dealings whatsoever with fetish priests or juju medicine men. For about one year he had no following at all; in fact people continued to make fun of him. After that following at all; in fact people continued to make fun of him. After that time, however, his preaching began to touch the hearts of some hearers, and they started coming to him. Soon the movement spread to other centres.

Samuel Brako died on 9th September 1946. On his death-bed he installed the present leader as his successor by placing his right hand upon his head and praying to God warmly three times in the presence of leading members, that god would give him all the spiritual powers necessary for leadership, and grant a continuing succession. He died immediately after finishing the third prayer. The man thus appointed to this office is Isaac Asirfi, the natural nephew and heir of the founder, whom he had carefully prepared for his responsibilities. He had taken him on preaching tours, and made him preach on several occasions; he let him take part in all important consultations with the elders, and when he made him conduct entirely the important camp revival meeting which was held at Agogo in the year before his death, it became an open secret within the group who the next head was going to be. This gentleman was, in 1958, about 40 years of age, and had four wives and six children, none of whom was as yet in school.

The official title of the leader here is Okyerekyereni (teacher) or Opanyin (elder). The word 'prophet' is not used because the present leader holds a poor view of some of those who so described themselves, and because, in any case, his predecessor had not adopted this designation.

Organization

This connection offers no remuneration any kind - money, goods, or services - to any of its leaders. The men appointed to head the local groups must be resident in the place concerned, and have their own means of stable livelihood. Most of them, including the Opanyin himself, are cocoa farmers, but there are many artisans too among them: carpenters, masons, smiths, tailors, etc., of the level of competence suitable for rural areas. With regard to remuneration of workers, the leader expressed the principle of the group to me in this way: 'With us, everybody must work, and do real work; if someone is without a job we find him one; if he will not work, he cannot be with us. This is the reason why we have no stealing here as is common at other places.' When asked whether those who lived by preaching only did not do 'real' work, he smiled and said that although this was good it would better still if preachers did something else as well.

The leaders of local branches bring all difficult maters relating to their congregations to headquarters for settlement or advice. They likewise report their difficulties in interpreting the Bible, and are told the Church's official explanation or doctrine on the point which may be at issue; they are under obligation to follow the line laid down at headquarters.

There are no special men or committees set aside to deal with these various matters and to supply the answers required, but all available elders meet as a family under the leadership of the Opanyin, as occasion demands, to discuss and decide upon the questions brought forward. No women are allowed at any of these meetings, but even quite small boys may be present, though, of course, they do not speak. The reason given is that God has placed women under the authority of men, and it is bad both for the women themselves and for the community as a whole if they are allowed to take up responsibilities which God never intended them to assume. A lot of disorder and confusion has been caused in other churches by giving places to women on councils. This is contrary to the law of God in Holy Scripture.

(It was quite obvious that this matter had been carefully thrashed out previously: not only was the answer ready and quite definite, it was also supported by a verbatim quotation from memory of 1 Tim. 2. 11-13 [in Twi],[1] and of parts of the beginning verses of 1 Cor. 1-11) [2]

The local leaders receive no formal training for their work. Some of them can read and write the local language; more can only read. The Opanyin himself can read Twi (not very fluently), but he cannot write it. Apart from his personal assistant, none knows English. Literacy is not considered as a condition for leadership, neither does it entitle its possessor to preferential treatment over others in this regard. Where a leader is illiterate someone else, often a schoolboy, is found to read the Bible to him, and he then expounds it.

The Opanyin visits sub-stations from time to time, to strengthen and encourage the members; these, on their part, occasionally come to headquarters for important meetings and celebrations, but also simply for the fellowship. No cash offerings are asked for, but foodstuffs are often collected for distribution to the aged, the sick, widows and orphans and others in need. Whenever money is required for a specific purpose, it is subscribed by members for that purpose only.

Religious Worship

Daily prayers are held at 4.30 am and at 7 pm. The main service of the week is on Saturday morning, and lasts from about 10 am to 12 noon. The one I attended was taken by the Opanyin himself; he usually conducts this service at headquarters. There was much hearty singing of African lyrics, begun by one person and joined in by the whole congregation. Several men made the start. No foreign melodies were sung. There were also three or four rounds of prayers, separated by singing. Again only men offered prayer. Each prayer was punctuated with many warmly-uttered 'Amens', said by the other worshippers. Considerable religious emotion was displayed, but it was not excessive. Men and women were present in about equal numbers, and there were many children. The women heartily joined in the proceedings: there was no sign that the official attitude on their position was about to call forth any demand for their 'rights.'

The leader made the exposition sitting at his table. His assistant read the passage 1 John 3. 1-10 from the Twi Bible verse by verse, and he commented upon it. He gave a good deal of general good advice for living, and dwelt especially upon the evil of any indulgence in alcohol. Much of this did not seem directly related to the passage or particularly significant. The exposition was combined with catechetical instruction. From time to time the leader threw out a question to the congregation at large, to be answered by any many who might wish to do so; at times he asked individual men what they thought of some point or another. On their part, members of the congregation would also interrupt to make comments or require further elucidation of some point which had been made. It was an informal and lively interchange in which all seemed to participate, though the women did so only as listeners. At its conclusion there was more singing, after which the service ended with the repetition by all (including women) of the Lord's Prayer, and benediction by the leader.

No footwear of any kind may be worn by anyone going into this church.

The Sacraments

Confession of sins and mutual forgiveness of offences must precede baptism and Holy Communion. I was told that on one occasion certain men, all ready to be baptized, had to withdraw because they were still entertaining some grudges that they would not let go. They were so shaken by the 'spiritual' prayers preceding the proposed ceremony that they begged for it not to go forward, and that they be given time first to put themselves to rights. Baptism is by total immersion three times in a running stream. One flows conveniently past the head station. There are two or three men specially set apart to perform this rite as occasion demands. Both adult and infant baptisms are practised. At the communion service, which is held from time to time, water is used instead of wine. Only the head of the Church administers communion.

The Methodist custom is followed, with slight adaptations, and there are no peculiar practices.

I witnessed the baptism of an infant. The baptizer took it from its mother, stripped it and standing in the middle of the stream, the baby held in his left arm while his right was lifted up, he offered a prayer. It was a good, orthodox Christian prayer: thanking God for the gift of the child, asking for it to be baptized with the Holy Spirit, and to be blessed of God for this life and for eternity. As he waxed eloquent he became more and more agitated, and soon began to shake in his whole body. At the height of emotion he broke into song, which was immediately caught up by the bystanders on the bank, and so movingly sung that some people came to tears. Then he stooped down and dipped the baby in the stream three times, all the body except the head; after that, scooping some water with his right hand, he washed its face and head. The child received an African name. He then walked up the bank and gave it back to its mother, and I heard him tell her to wrap it up well, so that it would not catch a chill. This ceremony was performed soon after noon, after the close of the main Saturday morning service.

Other Church Regulations

Polygamy is regarded as normal in this Church, and there is no restriction on the number of wives which a man may marry. The Opanyin explained that their concern was not how many wives a man had, but rather that he should be able to maintain peace, harmony and good order in his home and within his family. I found here, of all the places I visited, the greatest freedom and unawareness of any discomfort in the discussion of this matter of polygamy. From time immemorial, it was stated, the way of common decency was for a man to marry the women he fancied, as he was able, and not to go around deceiving girls, or meddling with other people's wives. And the Bible confirmed that. The idea that a man should marry one wife belonged to Europeans only; if they kept to it in their own country they were certainly not doing so in Ghana. How some Africans came to think that they should enslave themselves to European notions and why they should persist after seeing plainly that they were only being fooled, was a wonder, etc. It was spoiling the country for, because of it, women were getting more and more undependable. To the question whether it might be necessary for some restriction to be placed on the number each man may marry, in order that all should find wives, the answer was that our forefathers had no restrictions yet there had always been enough women to go round.

Regarding healing, the leader expressed himself as follows: 'My main work is not to heal but to preach. However, if people come for healing I receive them and pray for them. I always ask them first of all to confess the sins which they have committed, because every serious illness is caused by some sin. Occasionally we hold fasts to aid the prayers for healing.' (My assistant reported that he had claimed to be able to cure all sorts of maladies, and even to revive a dead person; but he made be such claims to me.)

Special Dress

The men wear long read gowns, some of them having on, as well, turbans of the same colour; for the women the colour is white, for both gowns and head kerchiefs. It is said that no symbolic significance whatever was attached either to the practice of wearing them or to the choice of colours. 'We only thought it would be a good thing to do because Our Lord Christ himself and his disciples were similarly dressed, as we have seen from the pictures of them.'

The Memeneda Gyidifo have no connection at all with Seventh Day Adventists or any other sabbatarian group within or outside the country.

[2]

In spite of several accretions, the Methodist background of this movement is unmistakeable, showing up clearly, as it does, both in the principal emphasis of the group, namely strict teetotalism (in Ghana temperance is a characteristic Methodist accent), and in their form of holding religious worship. Of the six men whom I asked how they came to join the Church, four answered to the effect that they used to drink heavily and, while fully aware that they were hurting themselves, they had been unable to refrain until they joined the group. One of these said with great emotion that through liquor he had become onipa hunu, i.e. a worthless person, but now, thanks to the prayers said for him in the Church, he was all right again; he felt strong in body and very happy in his mind, so he was going to live and die as a staunch member of this Church; the majority of the men in it had had similar experiences.

Of the remaining two, one said that he joined because he had seen what a happy fellowship the members had with one another; they were all respected in the town and although they never used foul language nor did they crack bad jokes, they seemed to be enjoying themselves even better than those who did. The life was a good one and he had every intention of always remaining a member. The last man questioned said that he used to spend a lot of money on medicines but never kept good health. Since he joined and prayers were said on his behalf, he had been perfectly fit. A woman stated to my assistant that she had been a prostitute, but had been reinstated by the Church as a respectable person. Most of the others who spoke to him gave healing from various illnesses as the reason for their joining. Those we saw did look healthy and vigorous; they were very responsive to simple jokes, and laughed with great heartiness.

The other rule said to be rigidly applied is that members may cohabit only with their own wives. If was reported that several had resigned their membership because they felt that these rules were too severe, and some had been excluded for offences in these matters, including a woman who had divorced her husband with the intention of marrying another man.

All members are expected to demonstrate their solidarity with one another in bereavement. At the funeral of a member, mourners may weep only quietly. The loud cries, and the singing, drumming and dancing (not to speak of the drinking) usual at funerals, particularly in the rural areas, are not permitted. The burial is carried out according to the Methodist rite, and one week afterwards, members call upon the bereaved to offer gifts to help toward paying their expenses.

There is here an interesting blend of the old and the new. The statements reported in regard to marriage and family life represent the old African ideal of a society well ordered in these respects. The group seeks to restore this state of affairs. Also, in common with practically all other sects and numerous new voluntary organizations, it is concerned to revive a measure of the old African community solidarity and mutual help. On the other hand, it is opposed to certain things which were also undeniably features of African life in the past, such as the free used of liquor and the traditional pattern of holding funerals. It must be presumed that these practices are rejected because they are held to be inconsonant with certain values after which the group aspires; in other words, there is more to the development than a simple desire of return to the past.

Notes

[1] 'Let a woman learn in silence with all submissiveness. I permit no woman to teach or to have authority over men; she is to keep silent. For Adam was formed first, then Eve.'

[2] '(3) But I want you to understand that the head of every man is Christ, the head of a woman is her husband, and the head of Christ is God ...(9) Neither was man created for woman, but woman for man.'

CHAPTER FIVE

Apostolowo Fe Dedefia Habobo
(The Apostolic Revelation Society)

[1]
THE headquarters of this Society is at Tadzewu in the Keta district of the Trans-Volta Region of Ghana. It is reached by road from two points on the main road from the Volta River at Sogakope to Denu, and also from Hevi on the Ho Denu road, being only 7 miles from this junction. The founder of the Society is Mr. Charles Kobla Nutonuti Wovenu, generally known as Prophet Wovenu, but regularly referred to by his followers as Mawu fe ame (i.e. man of God). The last name Wovenu, meaning literary 'He has received mercy,' was revealed to the prophet in a dream, in which he was instructed to make it his surname. Here is his own account of himself and of his work:[1]

'My father's name is Emmanuel Nutonuti, and my mother's Mikayanawo. Both were pagans when I was born. My father afterwards became a Christian, but my mother became a dasi (literally wife of a snake) i.e. a priestness of the snake fetish. My father remembers that, about 10 years before I was born, a stranger, dressed in a long, white gown, once lodged with him. My mother was then barren and remained so a long time, all medical and magical treatment having failed to help her; indeed I am her only child. Yet this man told my father that she would bear him a son, and that this son's head would stand higher (literally 'go further') than my father's.

'For this reason when I was born in December of 1918 (the day of the month is unknown), my father greatly disliked me. He thought that somehow my arrival signalized his own death, not knowing that the fortune-teller's prophecy merely meant that my religion would be a better one than his. I attended the Government Boys' School at Kibi from 1930 to 1935, living with my uncle Mr. Alfred Kpodo, who was working in that town. I afterwards came back to my home country to continue my schooling at Anyako, and I finished at the fifth standard under Teacher (now the Reverend) E.A. Banini. I became in turn a Post Office messenger, a policeman, a prison warder, an employee of the Government Department of Agriculture, and of the Mines office at Akwatia.

'Those who knew me from my infancy tell me that even as a child I used to be fond of "prophesying," and of doing signs and wonders, but I do not remember any of these things myself from that period.

When I was a warder of H.M. Prisons at Akuse, however, things like that used to happen. I used to be extremely fond of singing hymns and religious songs, and of praying aloud. My landlady, a certain Madam Aheyatowo, of Anloga, once called me and asked if anything was going wrong with me. When I answered in the negative, she said that she forbade me absolutely to be getting up so early in the morning and making such a noise with my singing and my praying. Although I promised to obey, the urge to sing and to pray in the early hours of the morning became quite irresistible. It was at that time (in 1934) that I also began to preach publicly. I used to preach to all who would listen, both at Akuse and at Amedeke. Strangely enough, even I myself did not understand what I was doing, neither did I really enjoy doing it. The whole thing was like as if someone were blowing into a horn, or like taking a journey in a dream before one wakes up again.

'I left Akuse to find new work in the diamond mines of Akwatia where I was engaged, in the first instance, as an unskilled labourer. I had a very hard time at the beginning and, not having done this kind of work before, my palms were soon full of blisters. But I comforted myself with singing and praying. God had mercy on me, and wanted to lift me up and to honour me. For this reason he illumined our supervisor, a Scotsman named Mr. Mac W. Smith, who one day asked me if I was literate. Upon learning that I was, he instructed the company carpenter to make a table for me, and showed me how to keep count of, and to record, the numbers of carts of diamond-laden earth that the labourers pushed in everyday. Everybody was surprised at my elevation, particularly as this post did not exist previously, and they were still more surprised when eventually I was transferred to the General Office as a full clerk.

'During my stay at Akwatia from 1935 to 1939 I preached a great deal, holding Bible classes, conducting a singing band, and even teaching literacy in my off-duty hours. I became even more interested in these activities than in the job for which I was paid. All over the district I was well known as a voluntary evangelistic worker. At the outbreak of the Second World War it was announced that all the employees of the mines would be regarded as conscripted, with the exception of the chief clerks only. This was not to my liking, so I left Akwatia to return to my hometown, Tadzewu.

'This town is reputed in the district for its market, to which people come from far-off places. But the inhabitants were very few when I arrived, some 150 to 200 people all told. The men were mostly farmers, who also tapped palm-trees for wine; the women sold palm-wine and various foodstuffs. The inhabitants were all very fond of drumming and dancing, but they used these recreations as occasions for singing mocking and insulting songs about one another, saying very bitter things to one another in pretendedly jocular fashion. In short, it was a vicious form of amusement, for which no good could come. Water was extremely hard to come by in the place. The shallow wells dug in the beds of streams soon dried up, and water had to be fetched by head porterage from distances of from 2 to 9 miles according to the severity of the drought. This difficulty was a major factor in preventing the growth and development of the town. It was surrounded on all sides by thick woods, and sanitation, in particular with regard to the disposal of all kinds of refuse, was at a very low level.

'Previous to my arrival, the Roman Catholic Mission had made attempts to establish a station there, but they had been so discouraged by conditions and the utter indifference of the local people that they had abandoned their efforts. There were only two Christians in the town when I arrived. They had been converted and baptized elsewhere before going there, but although they had not lapsed back into heathenism they showed little sign of being different from the rest of the people, having neither leader nor meeting place. The heathen gods then generally worshipped were Nyigbla, Afa, Yewe, Kunde, and the local stream, Tadze. There being no post office, the only means of sending messages to people elsewhere was to entrust them to those who happened to be travelling there, or to send one's own messenger or else to go personally. My father had the only shop in town; but Hausa itinerant traders also hawked some imported wares.

'I left Akwatia on the 4th of October 1939 but it was not until the 1st of November that I got home. Early the following morning, I sent someone round the town with a hand-bell to summon all who would come. There were many children and a few adults. I preached to them, and spoke to the children especially about the advantages of attending school. I asked if they would like to go to school, and they hailed the idea with great delight. On the following day, I had not myself even risen from bed before they began to foregather. There were 24 of them, and this was the nucleus of my school. I felt intensely happy, like a man, who had at long last found his real life's vocation.

'Apart from the school, I undertook some work among grown-ups too. I organized voluntary sanitary overseers to help promote cleanliness in the town; I also started a prayer group, with regular meetings for biblical exhortation and prayer. Although all the members were as yet heathen, I taught them to call on the name of Jehovah the great God, and on the name of Jesus Christ, and soon several among them were able themselves to offer Christian prayers both in public and in private. When I saw how well they were doing, I turned the group into a catechumen's class and had its members baptized when they were ready, by the Rev. Elias W. Tamakloe of the Ewe Presbyterian Church then stationed at Abor. These first Christians formed the mainstay of my work in the succeeding period, and continue to be such until the present day. In addition to my work in church and school I started a dispensary and dressing centre. My volunteer helpers and I dressed all sorts of sores, and I gave to the people, free of charge, many of the common patent drugs which they needed, and of which I kept a supply at my own expense. For all other sick I held regular sessions of prayers for healing.

'After I had been labouring in this way for two years, the Rev. E. W. Tamakloe suggested that my work should become part of the Ewe Presbyterian Church organization, and I agreed to this proposal. Upon his death the Rev. D. K. Ametewee took his place, and then the church laid down certain conditions for my continuing to work under its auspices. In the first place, I was to stop holding special prayer sessions for healing. Secondly, I was to make my schoolchildren pay fees as pupils did in other schools. I had started this school as an orphan school, knowing that for several of the keenest boys and girls any payment of fees was quite out of the question. The school used to do odd jobs for people, such as weeding their farms, tending their cattle, carrying water for them, etc., in order to earn, not only their schooling expenses, but also feeding and clothing for those who could not get even these from their own parents. Mr. N. C. Lawrence, the Government Education Department officer in charge of the district, also said that, in order that the children should not take undue advantage of my generosity in providing a non-fee-paying school, or be taken advantage of by being made to do more work than they received value for, or was good and proper for them to do as children, I should simply adopt the fee-paying system practised by all other schools, and avoid a lot of trouble for everybody.

'These conditions were unacceptable to me, so the Church and I parted company in 1945. There was unpleasantness because in the first place the church then tried to run a rival school, which failed completely and had to be given up; and secondly because of a grant of £85 which had been given to the school by the District Commissioner Mr. T. A. Mead. The Church claimed that this grant was intended for its own school because it was the one permitted by the Education Department, whereas the DC meant it for the school which he had actually seen, namely, mine. I still have all the unhappy correspondence on this matter in my files.

'I had many and great difficulties in building up and maintaining the school. The mud walls, built by the pupils themselves, would often crumble seriously during the rainy seasons, because we did not have sufficient help from adults skilled in thatching, when putting on the roof. Often we were attacked by white ants, which, during one night, would eat away practically all our furniture and our clothing. For a long time it was extremely difficult to find enough pupils, or to persuade them to stay, after I had trekked to far-distant villages to bring some. For three years (by which time there were six classes) I taught the whole school alone; from 1942 onwards I had the assistance of other teachers. However, since all I could pay them was ten shillings a month (apart from some farm products and services given to them), they came and went, and we could not have a stable staff.

'I was greatly encouraged in my difficulties by certain acts and promises of God. Through constant prayer, we overcame the attacks of the white ants. They eventually disappeared altogether, so that no one visiting our station today would think that they ever seriously troubled us. On 22nd August 1947 God spoke about the school as follows: "This school will not be a failure. Now it is entering upon its good times." Again on the 25th of May 1948 he said: "I shall cause to stumble those who ask: What can Wovenu do, and how can a good school come from him? Wovenu's work will spread to the south and to the west." On 1st June 1946 God spoke again and said: "I shall strengthen your works. Great doors will open for you. Your name, which was nothing before, shall now be very beautiful in their ears but you will have nothing to do with pride. Those who feed from your hand will be more than a thousand, and the town in which you live will have light. There will be bicycles in your gates, and many human beings shall lie round about. There will be an abundance of money in your house. O, where are now those who used to insult and mock you?"[2]

'Among many other revelations was one on 29th September 1946 to the effect that I would now have trained certificated teachers for my school. This prophecy came to pass in the arrival, on 28th September 1949, of Mr. A. A. Kuadey, followed soon afterwards by Mr. J. K. Tsa. As the school was still unrecognized by the Government, so that no grants were paid towards teachers' salaries, these men had to make do with very meagre salaries until 1952, when finally the school was placed on the list of schools encouraged by the Government.[3] For what God himself intends to do must needs happen.

'Both the town and the congregation also grew by leaps and bounds. There are about 1000 people in Tadzewu today, most of them strangers who have come here somehow or other in connection with my work. Among the aboriginal population Christians now greatly outnumber pagans, and only a few heathen rites are still to be seen being performed publicly. My Society has its own hospital, with accommodation for people who come from distant places for healing.[4] Those with contagious diseases such as leprosy, tuberculosis, epilepsy, yaws, various bad skin diseases and whooping cough are required to live separately. We have had two cases of smallpox that we promptly reported to the District Government Hospital, which immediately took charge of them. We engage in practising and teaching many useful trades and businesses. Apart from providing the income that we require, these occupations offer opportunities of apprenticeships and gainful employment to many of our young people. I run a poultry farm and vegetable gardens; corn-mills and lorry transport; workshops for tailoring, black smithy, the maintenance and repair of lorries and bicycles, etc. We have a post office, a printing press and electricity plant of our own. In our Society we support only genuine destitutes, all others have to fend for themselves.

'One of the greatest steps forward was taken when God in his mercy permitted me to ordain my own clergy to assist me in his work. On the of 19th June 1949 I ordained the first batch of these, 17 in number, with 4 "judges."[5] Since then their number has greatly increased, and not only have I benefited from their help, but I have had the joy of knowing that my work cannot now perish, for even if I should die, there are those who will carry it forward.

'One remarkable feature of our Society's life is the yearly great festival or "Anniversary." It lasts a whole week. Quite early in our history the members of the Society began to attach great importance to it, and even after seven days of celebrations nobody ever gets tired; always it is only with the greatest reluctance that people finally leave again to return to their own homes. Since 1954 we have organized the anniversaries with such care that each has been grander and better than the preceding one. Our spending for hospitality alone now exceeds 1000 pounds sterling on each occasion, but on the other hand people make generous voluntary offerings, so that a substantial part of the revenue of the Society comes from this source. Each celebration remains the talk of the whole district in which it was held, if not of the entire Trans-Volta Region, for weeks and even months afterwards.

'Our workers take no fixed salaries. We all share whatever funds are available from voluntary gifts, whenever it is convenient to do so. We likewise share the foodstuffs from our Society's farms, and at outstations members assist their workers by making and maintaining vegetable gardens for them. We all find that this is ample to meet our needs, and God always provides.

'There is no difference between our doctrine and that of the Ewe (now Evangelical) Presbyterian Church.[6] Our food taboos are those stated in the Old Testament. The official robes and other uniforms worn in the Society were designed by myself. They have no special significance. We practise fasting, but no general regulations have been laid down about it. It is left to each minister to know by himself when a fast is called for, and how severe it ought to be. He will judge that from the seriousness of the case in hand requiring a fast. On the whole we try to emphasize that Christian righteousness and brotherly love are more important than much fasting, but at times the latter is also necessary. Polygamy is allowed, according to the Scriptures, but not loose living in sexual matters. When a case of fornication has been confessed, the parties concerned are urged to marry, their parents and relatives, if members of the Society, being prevailed upon not to place unnecessary hindrances in the way. All cases of disorder or threatening quarrel among the members are settled by the "judges" appointed expressly for this purpose; in the most serious matters they sit together with the pastors and elders. There is no permanent excommunication of a member. A member may be temporarily excluded if he is found to be harbouring a bitter hatred.[7]

'Members of other Christian denominations may join our Society and still retain their membership in their own churches, but we do not accept pagans, Muslims or other non-Christians. Our instruction period both for adult baptism and confirmation is one year, but in cases of emergency, a person may be baptized after only two weeks of instruction. We recognize and practise infant baptism. In this rite, as in confirmation and the ordination of ministers, we follow the usage of the Evangelical Presbyterian Church, as adapted by ourselves.

'We print and distribute our own literature. Our hymnbook is the work of the printing firm of J.J. Augustin Gluckstadt in Germany. It was an unforgettable day of triumph and rejoicing when, at the great anniversary which we celebrated at Papase in 1953, this collection of our Society's own dearly beloved songs and hymns could be put in the hands of members as beautifully bound book. We have in booklet form the history of our Society from the beginnings till 1954. We print yearly calendars showing the Bible passages to be read by members and to be used for preaching every day of the year, as well as giving statistics and other important information about the current state of the Society. I used to have these printed by the Scottish Mission Press at Accra, but at one stage the Manager told me that the Evangelical Presbyterian Church had raised an objection, so I now have them printed by an independent African firm at Cape Coast.'

/2/

In 1958 this Society claimed around 50,000 members.[8] Its calendar for that year names 115 towns and villages in which it is represented; in 33 of them it had a school as well as a congregation. The number of ministers given is 55, but I was informed later on in the year that this had risen to 70. Besides 65 school-teachers and 3 'judges,' the following are listed as the official workers of the Society: office clerks, 5; herds-men, 4; printers 4(including 2 women); masons, 8; tailors and dressmakers, 5 (3 women); carpenters, 7; organist, 1; nurses, 9 (3 women); children's nurse, 1 (woman); labourers, 2 cornmill tenders, 3 (2 women); drivers, 3; blacksmiths, 3; mechanic, 1. This gives an indication of the Society's activities.

Under the heading 'Other Institutions or Agencies of the Society' the calendar shows: '1. Moral Institutions; 2. The Institute of Marriage Instruction (This is printed in capitals, doubtless to indicate the importance attached to it); 3. Community Centre; and 4. Trade School'. All these are located at the Tadzewu headquarters. I did not see the 'Moral Institute.' Probably, what is meant is the meetings organized to discuss married life and good behaviour in general. The 'Institute of Marriage Instruction' is a sort of boarding school for girls, run on lines similar to those of a convent. There were some 20 in residence at the time of my visit, their age ranging from about 13 to about 18. In charge was an educated, middle-aged widow from an urban area in the district, of very good family and upbringing; In fact it is she who holds the official position of organist, being an extremely competent and effective accompanist on the harmonium. The girls study all the various aspects of ordinary domestic science and childcare, as practised in the homes of educated but non-professional Africans. All the indications were that they received a good deal of moral exhortations as well. There is not a trade school as such but several boys living with the boarders of the elementary school or with families in the town learn their chosen trades as apprentices in the various workshops.

Some points in the instructions given in the calendar regarding correspondence with headquarters may be of interest: 'For 1. Requests for prayer; 2. Consultation of God; 3. Births; 4. Matters relating to death, write to the Recorder, A R Society ... If you wish the Man of God[9] to undertake some work for you, write to the ARS Ministry Office ... If you are only writing to him personally, address your letter to Prophet C. K. N. Wovenu, ... If you want any of the following things: 1. A complete building (i.e. to be constructed); 2. Kente cloth; 3, a cow, sheep, goat, or superior-breed ['European'] chicken, write to the Secretary, ARS Labour Party.'

The main purpose of the calendar is, however, to give the selected Bible readings for each day of the year, as well as Church statistics, etc. In the Preface the Prophet urges all members to buy copies because he had asked God especially to be directed to choose the most suitable and helpful passages, and because by so doing members would make it possible for him to continue to give them his services.

The Teaching of the Society

Although Prophet Wovenu believes that his doctrinal position is identical with that of the Evangelical Presbyterian Church, his is the only indigenous 'spiritual' group with a carefully worked out and printed catechism of its own at present. A copy of an official English version of this booklet (at present only in typescript) was supplied to me personally by the Prophet at my request, and is reproduced in the present study as Appendix C. 1. The original Ewe version also contains a fairly detailed plan for a six-year course of Religious Instruction in schools, with aids on the use of the scheme for catechumens as well. It further indicates the essential knowledge that must be required of members at various stages, etc. In this version (but not in the English) is also a statement on 'The Tasks of Wovenu's Appearance (or beginning).' I reproduce it hereunder in my own translation, because it appears to me to give a significant summary of the Prophet's own views regarding himself and his mission.

1. Prophet Wovenu has emerged as the warrior of righteousness against unrighteousness for the destruction of the kingdom of the enemy Satan upon earth; 2. Wovenu has appeared to restore ancient family houses that have become desolate, so that the glory and honour of God which was disappearing should make way for the Kingdom of God to come upon earth. Matt. 6. 10; 3. Prophet Wovenu has appeared as that proclaimer of the Gospel to whom God the Most High has entrusted the power of holy unction for the upbuilding (lit. correction) of holy men in hatred of sin, so that only the doing of good should prevail upon the earth. Heb. 1. 9; 4. Prophet Wovenu has appeared as a physician, to give recovery to all flesh that is groaning under illhealth; further he is a physician to all weak followers of Christ, for the steadfastness of their souls in God, according to his own strength and permission.

In this connection again it is interesting to note that the ten biographies to be studied by Sixth Year pupils are given as follows: 1. The Apostle

John (100); 2. John Chrysostom (347-407); 3. Augustine (354-430); 4. George I (540-605); 5. Winfred Bonifacio (680-755); 6. John Wycliffe (1320-1384); 7. John Hus (1373-1415); 8. Dr. Martin Luther (1483-1546); 9. David Livingstone (1813-1874); 10. The Apostle (sic) Charles Wovenu (1939 -).

Theological Education

At Tadzewu a long, swish-walled, zinc-roofed, unceilinged room bears, in very bold lettering, the words: 'The Theological College.' This Society is lucky in that a number of outstanding ex-Mission teacher-catechists have joined it, who are well able to undertake the instruction of their other colleagues. The Prophet himself is in charge of the College and is assisted by one or other of these men called in from time to time. The time-table shows 25 teaching periods per week, each of one hour's duration, distributed as follows: Scriptures 2; Music 2; General Education 2; Moral Education 1; Ministry 2; Management 1; Ethics and Etiquette 1; Building up of the Society 2; Copying 2; General Reading 2; General Discussion 1; Language Study 3; Religious Politics 1; Games 1; Groundwork 2.

Courses are organized and their duration is determined as convenient.

The Day's Activities at Tadzewu

The day starts with the ringing of the Boarding School bell at 4.30 am. In the School there is a short period of silent prayer, which is concluded with repetition of the Lord's Prayer aloud by all together. Then the school, as well as the entire station compound, is swept and cleaned, the boys have their baths and make ready for the day. At 6 am the main morning prayer is held. When I attended it on 18th December 1956 I counted just under 200 adults. As it is held at the sametime, so this service also takes the same form as morning prayer in the mother-church, the Evangelical Presbyterian Church: a hymn, prayer, Scripture lesson with short exhortation, prayer, concluding hymn and benediction. The service takes about half-an-hour, but most members like to stand around for a while after it, greeting one another and chatting a little, just as again is the custom in the mother-church. They finally disperse around 7 o'clock to begin the activities of the day.

In the Prophet's case, this means meeting at 8 o'clock with the elders and those in charge of the Society's various agencies and undertakings. From 9 am to noon on Mondays and Tuesdays he receives those who want appointments with him from various purposes, and if the matter cannot be disposed of at once, he arranges with them the time for taking on their individual cases. Most come with illnesses for healing, and dates and times are fixed for making special prayers for them, for anointing them, for fasting on their behalf, etc. Some come to ask that God be consulted for them with regard to particular concerns that they may have. Still others come to confess their sins and to obtain absolution. For minor matters, such must go to one or other of the 7 ministers resident at Headquarters (though, as these go on trek in the district, they are not all present at the same time); in serious cases involving others, the elders and available pastors sit together with the people concerned, to hear the confession and to take any action which they may consider necessary.

The 'consultations' proper are usually arranged for Wednesdays and Fridays, and in 1958 the Prophet estimated that he saw, on an average, 100 persons on each of those days. On Thursday mornings he attends to his correspondence and other private business, and on Saturdays he prepares himself for the Sunday.

At midday everyday there is a short public service of prayer on behalf of the sick. It is attended mainly by those who are living temporarily at Tadzewu to obtain healing. Attendance at this service by members of the Society as such is understood to be on a voluntary basis.

In the afternoons the Prophet makes his round of the sick and of the agencies. An evening service is held everyday from 8 to 9 pm, during which opportunity is given to members (in fact they are encouraged) to pray in public. After this service a team of up to five people (by a pre-arranged rota and either men only or women only) 'keep watch,' i.e. remain in constant prayer until midnight, when others join them for the 15-minute midnight service, which is the last of the day.

On Sundays there is the usual 4.30 am meditation, after which the announcements for the day are given out. The Children's Service is held at 7.30 am, and the main service of the week for adults from 10 am to 12 noon. From 4 to 6 pm there is either catechetical Bible study, or processions through the town, or a 'camp' service held in the open, or games and sports and other amusements. It is to be noted that the manner of holding these services is not different in any material respects from that of the mother-church, except that here there is more emotion displayed, though again not to anything like the same extent as in those church which aspire to ecstasy.

Teaching Praying in Public

The Prophet often expressed the importance of people abe to offer adequate prayers in public, believing this to be an essential part of their Chistian profession, and spoke of his efforts to teach both children and adults to do this. He taught them, he said, by offering a prayer himself and then calling upon the learners, in turn, to do likewise. One evening during one of my visits he assembled between 20 and 30 children, of ages between 5 and 10 years, to teach them how to pray. He ordered a huge basinful of boiled of boiled rice and corned-beef stew to be prepared for them, and the youngsters not only ate with great relish but also plainly overfed themselves. Then, after introducing me and telling them where I had come from, etc., he had them kneel in the cemented courtyard, offered a prayer himself and invited them to do the same. Several of the children prayed, some repeating much of the Prophet's prayer, and others making various little petitions of their own. I was quite nonplussed when on little imp piped up: 'Dear Father God, our stranger has come from very far. Please let him find what he is looking for. Amen!' Very soon, however, many were rolling over on the pavement in sleep, and little later, even the brave stickers became quite incoherent in what they were trying to say; so the session was brought to a close, and the youngsters were sent off to bed.

The Anniversary Celebrations
These are held towards the end of the year, usually at headquarters, but also at one or other of the main centres of the Society's work. Each celebration, beginning on a Friday, lasts one full week, but the highlight of the occasion is on the Sunday. I attended this main service in 1957. The programme for the two previous days had been as follows: 'Friday: 20th December 1957 10 pm Prayers and Watchnight. Saturday 21st ... Morning Service. Field Prayers and Benedictions. Thanksgiving service on behalf of the following: (a) The Electric Plant; (b) Donations from all well-wishers; (c) Other good works.'

On the Sunday the streets of the town were astir with crowds from the very early hours of the morning as women and girls fetched water, and boys ran around with newly-pressed clothes, or carried chairs, benches and school-desks to the place of meeting. Striking among the crowds were some lads and a few older men in uniform: khaki shorts and 'bush shirts,' with puttees, red cummerbunds, belt and cross belt, and cap. Some were on duty directing traffic in front of the Prophet's house and at other points in the town, there being quite a few lorries about that morning, bringing in the festival guests from distant places. Theses youths had a smart turnout and bearing, and seemed to be very conscious of their own importance, the gait of most of them being a real swagger.

Soon after 8 am the people began to assemble under the very large shed of palm branches, about 200 feet square, which had been erected for the meeting. At about 8.30 the uniformed men, some 20-30 of them, made a formation and began to march up and down the main street of the station, their 'officer' marching in front. This man had obviously had military or police training, because he was doing his part extremely well. Doubtless he trained the rest. He was wearing a special and very remarkable uniform, and the whole was quite a sight. As the band paraded it sang in Ewe a song which translates as follows:

> 'Let us go to Tadzewu
> In order to learn
> The reason why the Man of God
> Wants our presence there.'

They kept this up for over two hours, and even then did not look too tired. I learnt afterwards that they were called 'The Young Men' or 'The Soldiers,' and that their duty was solely to maintain good order among the festival crowds.

Also very much in evidence was the local Choir robed in flaming red surplices worn over white gowns, with scarlet caps. From several directions round about came various melodies as each visiting singing group or brass band marched through the streets on their way to the meeting place. It was a happy, festive commotion. By about 9.30 o'clock, the majority of the worshippers had settled down respectively in their various marked sections under the shed. At this time about 50 of the priests marched up, each man uniformed in a flowing white cassock with two red stripes on the neckband. They were officered by one of their number, and this was their marching song:

> 'Wovenu is building this new city
> For children of freedom alone.
> Therefore sing with a loud voice
> "Hurrah!" to Wovenu!
> "Hurrah! Hurrah! Hurrah!"
> "Hurrah!" to Wovenu!'

My estimate of about 5,000 for the number of the crowd was confirmed separately by two Central Government police whom I asked. People had come from all parts of the Trans-Volta Region, from the Eastern Region, and from the Republic of Togoland. As the Prophet was long in coming, the assembly was treated to a performance by a rural brass band which, with vocalist and loudspeaker in nightclub style, murdered the familiar tune 'Crimond' to the accompaniment of drums. The vocalist used the text of a well-known Mission hymn. After this had been going on for sometime, one of the singing groups simply broke in with a song, and the brass band had to stop.

At long last, well after 10.30 in the morning, the Prophet arrived, escorted by three European guests, merchants from Accra, with whom the Prophet had some commercial business and whom he had invited to the festival. Whilst he himself was dressed in a gorgeous ceremonial robe of rich yellow silk with red stripes on the neckband,[10] his friends wore only work-a-day shorts and shirts, and looked somewhat ill at ease. Arrangements under the shed were such that the Prophet sat in splendid isolation, the people nearest to him being not less than about 40 feet away. He had a microphone to himself, and very gaudy gold-coloured glass cross stood on the table in front of him. It began to drizzle. The Prophet reminded the assembly that traditionally rain on a high occasion was understood to signify the approval and the blessing of God.

After the usual preliminaries he preached a sermon in Ewe, which was translated into Twi for the benefit of the strong contingent present from the Buem country, where Twi is spoken. An English translation was also read. The translator spoke into a second microphone, placed at some distant from where the Prophet was sitting. The sermon, which the Prophet read from a typescript, was thoroughly orthodox, based upon the story of David sparing the life of Saul, it dwelt upon the danger to Christians of harbouring ill-feelings against others and rejoicing at their downfall. The rain came steadily harder as the sermon proceeded, and by the time the latter came to an end it was pouring, and everybody was badly soaked. The rest of the programme for the service had to be abandoned. Suddenly the Prophet, doubtless having in mind the fact that but for his late arrival the service as planned would have been completed before the coming of the rain, stood up and, disarmingly and with apparent candour, declared that he was a human being and a sinner, that he had sinned gravely that morning against God and against all the people of the Society present and absent by arriving so late; that God would forgive him for his sin; and proceeded to recite a few of the verses of the 51st Psalm. Thereupon the assembly dispersed, in a mood very different from that in which they had come together, and dripping wet.

I was unable to stay on for the grand procession planned for the afternoon, but heard afterwards that it was a great success. The remaining days of the anniversary were, according to the programme, to be devoted mainly to hearing reports from the districts, and to personal testimonies, as well as to various demonstrations. I learnt that all went very well.

[3]

The article on this Society already referred to (African World for July 1957) concludes with this comment: 'It is a very efficient organization indeed and a telling example of self-help which is bringing health and salvation to many Ghanaians.' Apart from its central interest of religion, Prophet Wovenu's movement undoubtedly has a very strong emphasis on 'progress,' i.e. the advance towards modern Western civilization, combined with good works.

He has had considerable success in realizing what many a 'Self-improvement Society' and local 'Scholars' Union' up and down the country has, during the last fifty years or so, set down in solemn resolutions as its aims and objects in respect of its 'beloved home-country.' This became so much the fashion that practically no district was without such an association of its own, but alas in most cases the high patriotic sentiments proved to be fleeting and nothing ever happened.

That this interest is intrinsic to Prophet Wovenu's movement and not merely a side-line or after-thought is shown not only by the fact that he never leaves out reference to it in any discussion of his work, but also that an item in the original vernacular version of his catechism is devoted to it. As this does not appear in the English version, I reproduce it in my own translation as Appendix C.2.

The general atmosphere at Tadzewu would strongly remind any ex-pupil of the old Bremen Mission central school at Keta of his childhood days. The movements, activities and customs of the people round about, the general ordering of the day, the prayer services at day-break and in the evening, the snatches of familiar tunes which catch the ear as they are whistled by some passer-by or played on a fife by some school-boy, or sung by some woman at her work – all are so very much like the past that one is assailed by a strong nostalgia. The way of life of this place is in fact more in continuity with that of the old days than is the one of the present official Church station at the same spot. Again, such an organization as the 'Institute for Marriage Instruction' is in direct line of descent from the practice of missionary wives in the pre-World War I days, to take in girls about reach marriageable age, for practical training in housecraft and Christian living. In my opinion, this service went much further than formal education in introducing the Christian way of home life among the people. That there is still clamant need for some such arrangement is clear from the fact that in the rural areas schoolgirls get little or no domestic science training at all, and that in any case they learn much better by doing than from class instruction.

It is noteworthy that, although Prophet Wovenu recounts several dreams and visions which were significant to him, he does not claim any specific call to his mission. Similarly, when asked for examples of dramatic miraculous cures, he said that he had not experienced any: even spiritual healing was usually a slow process, and there might even be set-backs at times; but in many cases full restoration of health was eventually achieved, and that was the important thing. This prophet freely uses all patent drugs and 'common medicines' known to him and available, though he emphasizes that the essential element in curing disease is intense supplication, with fastings, if necessary, on behalf of the patient, as well as by himself.

On the other hand, the devotion to him on the part of a great many of his followers is such as to lead to what practically amounts to a personality cult. His friends emphasize how he had not only brought healing to many but has been extremely generous to those in urgent material need, and zealous to assist the unemployed in finding a means of livelihood, etc. This appreciation of his helpfulness is attested by the fact that he is constantly receiving valuable presents and a considerable amount of unpaid or not fully paid services. The article already referred to contains these passages relevant to the discussion at this point: 'At Tadzewu the prophet is erecting a large concrete two-storey house. "We have no regular or visible means of income; but, thanks to God, we are steadily building the house. It is the Lord who is building it," he said. Among the many people he has cured are masons, carpenters, and other artisans who do not wish to leave him, and some of these are working on the house voluntarily. Occasionally the prophet gives them what money he can afford ... A short distance away were several young men, students of the theological school (elsewhere in the article their number is given as about 20), breaking stones for the building of the prophet's house. It is a voluntary service which they turn to any time they feel like it.'

I myself had experience at this place of an attitude towards money which I have hardly met anywhere else. I was to be travelling by car for several weeks, and wanted to hire a young apprentice from the Motor Repairs shop to accompany me. When I asked the young man what wages he wanted, he said that if I was going to give him his daily bread, then what we ought to be doing was to be praying to God for safety and for the successful carrying out of my business, rather than discussing money. At the conclusion of our journeys, all he would ask for was an old, discarded suit of mine, and his fare back. Of course on my part I insisted upon giving him all that he was due; he seemed to be alarmed at the amount at first but was, after a while, persuaded to take it.

Polygamy is allowed in the Apostolic Revelation Society, and there is no declared limit to the number of wives permitted. Not a word is said on this matter in the catechism, although the subject of marriage is treated; besides, not only the prophet himself but also his leading assistants showed the greatest reluctance to discuss this topic beyond admitting that polygamy was allowed.

'The prophet's attitude towards his mother-church, the Evangelical Presbyterian Church, is not easy to define. He speaks of it in a non-committal way, and yet leaves a vague impression that he has a sense of having been wronged by the Church. I believe that this came out unmistakably when he spoke of the Church stopping the Scottish Mission

Press from doing printing jobs for him. On the other hand, however, at the centenary celebration of the Church's station at nearby Anyako, it was the prophet's gift that was the largest single contribution, i.e. the sum of fifty guineas.

In the practice of 'camp' activities, the prophet is probably following the African Methodist Episcopal Zion Mission, which is represented in the area, rather than the older indigenous 'spiritual' churches such as the Musama Disco Christo. Both of them have this institution, but the approach of the latter group is far more emotional than that of the former.

NOTES

[1] This account is a conflation of information personally communicated to me by the prophet in a personal interview and material contained in a little booklet in Ewe by him on the history of his Society form 1939 to 1954: Apostolowo Fe Dedefia Habobo Nutinya 1930-1954, Mfantsiman Press Ltd, Cape Coast. As I had read the booklet before the interview, it was possible to ask for further elucidation on certain points.
[2] The phraseology of theses utterances is assimilated as much as possible to that of Old Testament prophecies.
[3] The prophet had now conformed to the regulations.
[4] This place is not to be conceived as a hospital in the usual sense. It merely consists of a number of huts in which the patients live, looked after by their own people under the supervision of the Society's nurses. These, though not professionally trained, can direct patients to take the drugs being used for them at the proper times, etc., and on the whole nurse the sick in a more enlightened way than their own people are usually able to do.
[5] The 'judges' are men (usually 3 or 4 in number) who are appointed to sit with the prophet and determine all matters threatening the peace, good order and harmony of the community.
[6] This assertion is discussed in Section 2 of this chapter.
[7] I think that this is an original and very significant point.
[8] The membership figure was given me by the prophet; the others are mostly taken from the latest available pocket calendar of the Society. The article in the African World states: 'Its active membership has reached a total of more than 60,000, and there are about 150 congregations or stations with primary schools attached, and supervised by 52 pastors of the Society.'
[9] This is the title used in Ewe, and not the word for a prophet such as the Old Testament ones.
[10] The prophet personally designed all uniforms in use in the Society. He said that there was no sort of significance attached to them.

CHAPTER SIX

Etodome Nyanyuie-Presbiteria Hame Gbedoda Kple Doyo-Habobo
(The Prayer and Healing Group of the Evangelical Presbyterian Church at Etodome)

[1]

UP The steep and wooded hillside to the north of the village school playing-ground at Etodome, near Hlefi, on the Anyirawase-Kpedze road in the Trans-Volta Region of Ghana winds a fairly broad and well-cleaned path, lined on both sides with ornamental plants. At the first turning in the path is a white-painted signboard bearing the inscription 'II Tim. 3. 14-17.' The other biblical references similarly displayed at the following turnings are, in order: '1 Peter 2, 21-25;' 'John, 14, 1-6;' 'Matt. 11, 28-30;' 'Luke 9, 23-24.' Beyond the fifth turning is a clearing in the bush terraced in five tiers, surmounted by a simple cross in cement. The place is planted with flowers and also furnished with a few benches. The local people call it Todzi (hill-top). It is used by the Etodome congregation of the EP Church for holding open-air services of worship and prayer on the first Sunday of every month, and by the Prayer and Healing Group very frequently for the same purposes as well as for meditation and private devotions, held individually or in small groups.

It was at this place of retreat that, in January of 1957, the founder and leader of the Prayer and Healing Group, replying to many questions, gave the following account of his life and of the experiences which had led to the formation of the group.

'My name is Frank Kwadzo Do, and I hold the position of Nunola, i.e. "Leader" within the group. I was born at Etodome about 1910. I went to live with my uncle, Hospital Dispenser Do, at Lome, where I was sent to school. The late Pastor Aku baptized me at Lome on 18th December 1915. I was at school from 1918 to 1927, finishing at Palime, to which place my uncle had been transferred. Then I was sent to Keta to be apprenticed to Messrs Alfred Lawson and Lassey, to learn the brick-laying trade.

'At the Palime School, scripture lessons in the upper classes were taken by Pastor Quist. One day towards the end of the school year, during the scripture period, he asked a number of boys what careers they wished to follow in life. He did not ask me anything, but at the close of the period, just before he left the room, he threw me a small Bible, saying that that should be my dowonu, i.e. "working tool" in life. I did not think of this incident much at the time, as I was going to learn to become a mason.

'After 3 ½ years of apprenticeship I successfully completed my course, and soon found my first job with the French Togoland Government. I was employed in constructing wells and in doing other masonry work in rural areas, and soon attained a position of some responsibility. Then one day Mr. Kelly, District Commissioner at Ho, came and asked the French authorities if they would spare me to come over to British Togoland to do there the same things as I was doing for them. I was released and re-employed at Ho, where I built the present retaining walls of the marketplace, and also dug some wells. I was afterwards sent to the Kpetoe area on similar assignments. Then I was transferred from Government service to that of the Asogli State, and was stationed by the latter at Ziofe to dig wells in that town and in the surrounding area.

'While at Ziofe I and some other members of the Evangelical (then Ewe) Presbyterian Church used to go to Dzalele to attend services on Sundays. It is a long way to walk and we used to feel excessively hot. Eventually I suggested that we might have services where we lived, and thought that, since I had held services before in my own hometown I could do so there also. We received permission from Mr. Bernard Attipoe to use the large verandah of his house for our services. At the first service the people could not sing the hymns which I called from the church hymnbook, so I asked them all to come again in the afternoon for hymn practice.

'To this hymn practice on the first Sunday of our Ziofe meetings was brought also, carried on the back of one of his aunts, a young son of Bernard Attipoe's named Togbui. The child became very ill and grew steadily worse; suddenly he stiffened, his eyes turned, and he seemed about to die. In fact I might say that he was even then already dead. I was most terribly upset, saying to myself that even if I had been wrong in bringing about this change in our place of worship, was it not too hard for God to show His disapproval by allowing such a great disaster to happen in connection with what we had started? I felt strongly that we should all kneel down and pray for the boy to be restored to life, and I called upon the whole assembly to let us do so. A man who after this event joined the Apostolic Revelation Society, Mr. Emmanuel Voegbolo, was also present.

'We all prayed most fervently, saying that if what we had undertaken was wrong, God would show us our error in another way; above all, that God would demonstrated his power in coming to our aid and vindicating himself and us before all those heathen people. When we had done with praying, I felt a great urge to anoint the child. I did this, and he seemed to improve slightly. I anointed him a second time, and then I felt strongly that I should throw my handkerchief on him. As soon as I had done that, the child visibly recovered, and stood up. He was sked what had gone wrong with him. He said, "Nothing," but that he was very hungry and wanted to eat. Then he walked straight up to me, and threw himself in my arms, at the same time urinating on my clothes. The food (akple) prepared for him was brought; he ate it and became altogether normal again. By this time the house was filled with a very large crowd of the townspeople, and great was their amazement at what had happened. I felt unspeakably grateful to almighty God because he had listened to us and not put us to shame. We prayed again, and I announced that there would be a special evening service of thanksgiving and praise for this great deliverance. This was the beginning of my present healing activity.

'At that time Wovenu of the Apostolic Revelation Society had already started his work of divine healing. Someone wrote to him informing him of what had happened, and he came there the very next day to enquire further about it. He asked me by what power I had healed the child. I told him that I had nothing apart from the Ewe Bible and prayer. He asked me what religious customs I practised, and I said none, except that I never committed adultery, and felt strongly that the day I would do so I would go mad. He said that that was a hard custom, but all the same he wanted me to join forces with him. I declined. Soon afterwards I was transferred from the area, and the Evangelical Presbyterian Church sent a teacher-catechist to take over the group of Christians which I had gathered and led while I was there.

'It was not long after this that I began to see visions. I had asked God in prayer for them. I had thought a lot about God's wish that we should consult him in all that we did. He himself had forbidden any dealing with fetish priests, medicine-men and all the other oracles that people normally consult. I felt it keenly as an unbearable lack that there should be no place to which people could properly turn when they wanted to know about themselves, their loved ones and their affairs. In II Kings 1. 6 [1] God asked the king whether it was because there was no God in Israel that he was sending to consult the oracle of Baalzebub, the god of Ekron? I came to the conclusion that, if asked, God would himself supply all the knowledge that people needed to have.

'The first vision I saw was of twin babies being born to my brother, Presbyter Win of Etodome. One was fair and the other was dark. In the vision I saw also that their mother's left breast was not yielding any milk, and I was told that through me God would cause that breast to flow with milk naturally, as a witness and a sign.

'I was living at Ho at the time, but I came to my hometown regularly every weekend to preach on the Sunday. I had no other information about the birth of the twins. In my vision I was told to let my daughter Laura take the sick breast on a white napkin in her left hand and rub it three times with a locally common flower which some people call "snowdrop." This was done in open divine service in broad daylight, and immediately afterwards the milk began to flow from the breast freely. Never was there any more trouble from that breast until the twins were weaned. Since that time I have had visions.

'Sometimes the scene is enacted before my eyes as on a cinema screen; sometimes I hear voices telling me of future or secret things and events. Sometimes when a patient is coming for healing by our group I feel it. These visions and voices come by themselves sometimes, at other times they come upon my request in prayer. Often visions come in a form which has to be interpreted. For example, in the case of the young woman whom I told yesterday that her marriage would not prosper, what I saw when she came forward was herself sitting under a wide-spreading tree, but the tree was withered and had no green leaves, only dried-up branches. Again, in the case of the driver's wife who had lost two children previously and is now expecting a third, whom I told that if her children had not died her husband himself would have died, what I saw was this woman, sitting in a widow's garb (a short black cloth), her hair entirely shorn,[2] roasting plantains; on her lap was a bonny, lively child. The meaning is that, with a living child she would have been a widow.

'I started healing since the case of my brother's twins. While I was at Kpeve I stayed in the same house as a cousin of mine, who was a member of one of the prophetic groups. I saw a letter written by their leader in which the latter described himself as "King of Light." I was so greatly agitated by this presumption that I could not rest until I had written to him saying that it was unthinkable for any human to write such a thing about himself, let alone a man who was married to nine wives and had said that he was going to have 17 or 19. He wrote back a 5-sheet reply, but it was all common abuse and did not answer any of the points which I had raised. He has since forbidden his people to come anywhere near me. I saw this man in a vision like a withered tree which has been choked by many adventitious roots. These represent his many wives. His movement is not a genuine thing.

'We are not highly organized, but simply make what arrangements are necessary as occasion demands. Mr. Erasmus Motte can take my place during my absence. He also receives visions. Mr. Traugott Keti can likewise act, though he does not receive visions. We have a committee of seven elders according to the Book of Acts.[3] Some of them see visions and dream significant dreams. Before doing anything, we ask in prayer for guidance; by this means we also often detect liars. Three times a year we hold a general meeting here of all members, lasting three days. We engage in mutual exhortation and encouragement, in the study of Scripture, particularly of the passages relating to healing, and to the activities of the Apostles. Above all we pray a great deal, and special requests for prayers in respect of difficult local situations, or of individual cases of suffering, are attended to. Formerly there were no women in our society, but now we admit women and hold courses of study for them in Christian womanhood.

'We practise fasting, and our days for doing so are Tuesdays and Fridays. We were led to set aside these two days and have no other reasons for this choice. Patients are required to fast up to 2 pm only, their relatives and those interested in them, as well as all others connected with our work here at Etodome, until 4 pm. On the first Tuesday of every month all our members in the country, no matter where they may happen to find themselves, must observe a fast until 4 pm. It was revealed to me that we should do so, and I can give no other reason.

'No footwear of any kind can be taken into our house of prayer. This is God's law, made plain without any possibility of useful controversy over it, by the biblical example of Moses and the burning bush.

'No cloth used at night in a matrimonial bed may be worn to the house of prayer, for this is an abomination before the Lord. Men and women should honour God by appearing before him and addressing him only in garments which are clean in every way.

'Likewise, no woman is permitted to enter the house of prayer during her monthly period. Long ago once my wife cooked for me during her period, and I had dreams of seeing the most revolting abominations and filth, things altogether so repugnant that I was not able to bear the sight of them. I learnt from this experience once for all that a woman in this condition is in fact unclean. At present my daughter Laura cooks for me (her age is about 18 years), but during her periods I manage on my own, and it is no hardship at all. It is not worth anybody's while to eat food cooked by a woman in such circumstances for any reason whatsoever.

'With regard to drugs, we use simple, patent ones bought from the stores, and African herbs well known and proved to be medicinally effective. But we regard drugs really as a means of giving encouragement to patients. It is in fact their faith that cures them. God has indeed provided herbs with healing efficacy, and of course he means men to use them to help themselves when they are sick. But they are merely secondary in healing, and with all their curative powers one may easily die in spite of their use.

'In the matter of speaking with "tongues," when I pray in that manner I do not myself understand what I say. I simply follow an impelling urge to utter these words, and I feel sure that the Spirit works through them, since they come from him. The Scripture says: "For one who speaks in a tongue speaks not to men but to God; for no one understands him, but he utters mysteries in the Spirit. On the other hand, he who prophesies speaks to men for their upbuilding and encouragement and consolation."[4] This is the way in which it started with me:

'Florencia Foli of Tongo once fell into a trance and remained in that condition for five days. She was brought to me after work on a Saturday afternoon at about 5 o'clock. She was quite stiff and unable to talk. When after my prayers on her behalf she began to come round, she first spoke in "tongues." I remember well that the particular Saturday in question was "pay-day."[5] Before she was brought I had had a vision that I and another man were trying to draw water from a well; the pail of the other man slipped and fell back into the well, whereas mine came out safely with lovely, sparkling water. I understood this to mean that the young woman's father Foli and I were both trying to save her life, but whereas he would fail I would succeed. Florencia afterwards told me that from that time onward the Lord would speak with me in "tongues," and this has been the case. This girl is also able to see visions. Once she saw one in which she was told to fast for ten days; she did so with greatly beneficial results in respect of her health and of her affairs in life generally.

'Regarding the interpretation of visions, there is nothing to be learnt about it; you just feel what the meaning must be, and you do not think of any alternative interpretations. If, for instance, in the case of a married couple you see a palm tree before you and it is withered, then you would know without a doubt that the husband will not overshadow (i.e. comfort and shelter) his wife. If the tree is green and flourishing, then, of course, he will, and there will be success in the marriage.

'Any communicant member of the Evangelical Presbyterian Church may be admitted to the fellowship of our group. No children can be members. We shall remain a part of the Evangelical Presbyterian Church as long as the Church authorities let us. We do not administer the sacraments on our own, and we have no special courses of training apart from intensive study of the Bible. Those who join us participate in what we do and that is all the training that they require. We do not accept non-Christians into membership, but Christians of other denominations than our own may join us if they wish to do so, and still retain fully their connection with their church if only their own authorities so permit. No dues are paid, but whenever it is necessary to raise funds for any purpose we do communal labour to find the amount of money required. I myself live by the thankofferings which people give me. After resigning from my employment as a Local Authority mason I used to cultivate my garden, but so many people come to me nowadays that it is impossible for me to do anything else. We demand from our members strict adherence to the principles of Christian living. If they mean business with it, they are welcome to come and to stay; otherwise, they need not come at all, or if they have come they need not stay. We have no interest in attracting large numbers of indifferent or half-hearted Christians. The total number of our members at present is about 100 men and 180 women, though we have helped many thousands of people.'

[2]
The Etodome group has a full and very busy week, each day being set apart for specific tasks as follows:

On *Mondays* non-resident expectant mothers are received. It is significant they are so many that a whole day must be given to them. They are anointed, advised on the use of various local plants considered in African herbal treatment to be helpful in pre-natal cases, and given consecrated water for use at home both in drinking and in rubbing the abdomen. Tuesdays are entirely devoted to in-patients who live in huts which either they themselves or their relative have built, or which they have obtained from previous patients. It is very temporary housing, the huts being practically all made of matted palm stalks and leaves, though there are a few with swish walls. These constructions, neatly arranged and kept scrupulously clean, cover between 1 and 2 acres of land belonging to the leader's family, and the whole place is called Bethesda Tato (i.e. 'On the shores of the Lake of Bethesda'). The session for prayers and intercession lasts some eight hours, beginning at about 8am, and all participants have to fast, patients up to about noon only, if they are judged to be weak; their relatives and friends, as well as the healers, up to about 4 pm. On Wednesdays outpatient children, and on Thursday outpatient adults, are seen for all complaints. On Fridays the healers, assistants and nurses hold a retreat, with fasting till 2 pm. Saturdays are free for gardening and domestic duties, and on Sundays public divine service is attended, morning and afternoon, sometimes (usually during moonlight) in the evening as well.

The weekday exercises are performed with such intensity that a feeling of exhaustion is very evident in the active participants when they have finished. The leader told me that sometimes he simply has to go away elsewhere to rest a little, otherwise the strain would be too much for him.

A short description of what happened on a day considered to be typical for each of the main functions should help to fill out the picture. The chapel or meeting place of the group is a thatch-roofed mud house measuring about 30 feet by 15 feet. The mud floor, the unworked tree-trunks used as beams and benches, the un-professional workmanship and finish give evidence of the use of both local materials and talent. A neat cement railing separating the leaders' section of the room from that of the people, reminds one that the founder is a trained mason. This whole section is raised about 10 inches, and cemented. The structure lies east to west. There are two small rooms in each corner of the east side, the space left between them being occupied by the altar. One room is for robing, the other for storing odds and ends. The altar is covered with a white cloth, upon which is placed a simple wooden cross flanked on either side by a candle. There are also a couple of carved ornamental pineapples. On the wall above the altar hangs a crucifix. In the leaders' section is a stand with a large jug of water, some empty jam bottles and a saucer with some salt in it.

On a Monday. Some 40-50 pregnant women were gathered in the chapel. Their heads were covered with the second (or 'free') cover cloth used in Ghanaian dress for adult women, although they all had on the usual headherchiefs as well. Apparently it was strictly forbidden for any hair to show, as one of the assistants went up to a woman and carefully covered a bit of her hair that had been protruding on her temple. All footwear must be left at the entrance of the chapel.

After greeting the assembly the leader invited the women to confess their sins, so that their prayers might be heard. One of them after another publicly said what she considered herself to have done wrong. The husband of the first speaker had deliberately angered her for no good reason, but had afterwards sent her twenty shillings; she felt very strongly that she should return the money to him. She was advised not to do so, and to have patience.

Several similar petty little matters were aired in this way, giving the leader opportunity to offer some common-sense general moral counsel. Since men were so easily led to follow women other than their own wives, the wives should pray for them incessantly; in a household the woman was more important than the man because if he was absent, nobody noticed it, whereas if the woman was absent the house immediately became empty. Patience and other womanly virtues should be cultivated.

When the confessions ceased, the leader arose, went into the robing room and soon emerged again in a long flowing white robe with an ornamented cape. He called a hymn from the Evangelical Presbyterian Church hymnary, which was heartily sung by most. Then he said a longish prayer invoking God's presence and support for the undertakings of the day, whereupon there was some more hymn singing. He next read and expounded John 1. 12, 13.[6] Those 'born of God' he declared to be those whose parents fulfilled God's law by going through the various processes necessary for a decent marriage, before having them. It was not necessary to have an expensive wedding with feasting, in fact it was bad to waste money in this way; but it was necessary to have God's blessing on the marriage pronounced by the minister, and it was also necessary that the couple should have their simple rings, the symbol of their union, blessed by the Minster. All this could take place quietly in the minister's study, with only two or three elders or church mothers present, but it gave honour to God and man, and made all the difference in the character of the children born. Those 'born of the flesh' were those born outside wedlock. They turn out to be rotten persons because they inherit the mood of immorality in which their parents had begotten them. The present increase in hooliganism and worthlessness was largely due to the disregard of all that was proper and befitting in marriage. We were far worse than our predecessors in this respect because, if they were polygamists, at least they took care to do what they did in the proper way; however, whereas we were being taught to do better than they and adopt monogamy and its pattern of family life, our response was rather to go in the opposite direction towards complete licence. This was a root cause of much sickness, and called for deep repentance and amelioration of our ways. The exhortation ended with the singing of another hymn.

The leader then told the assembly that during the first part of the intercessory prayers, when he would be praying for them in 'tongues,' they should accompany him with their own prayers in the local language, asking solely for the forgiveness of all their sins. This was done, all kneeling to pray. The leader then said that during the second part of the prayers, to be held similarly to the first, the patients should state clearly, specifically and fully, just what their trouble was, and what they wanted the Lord to do for them. Again this was done, everybody speaking at the same time, audibly but not too loudly, while the leader's voice predominated in the language of 'other tongues.' The benediction at the end was said in the local language, and included words to the effect that a healthy (lit. perfect) spirit should reside in a healthy body (Luvo deblibo nano nutila deblibo me, i.e. 'mens sana' etc).

The next stage was the conversion of the water in the glass jar into healing water. While salt was being gradually poured into the water, the biblical passage about Elisha changing salt water into sweet (i.e. 'healing' the water), and the verse 'For every one shall be salted with fire, and every sacrifice shall be salted with salt' (Mark 9. 49) were being recited, the pouring of the salt finishing on the last words of the latter text. This was followed with more prayer in 'tongues.' The women now came forward one by one and knelt before the leader. Repeatedly they had to be told to kneel 'upright,' i.e. not to bend the body at the waist. The leader asked the following and similar questions of them: 'What is your name? How many months old is the conception? How are you feeling? Do you have any pains? Do you attend Holy Communion?' If the answer to this last question was No, the patient had to explain why, and was exhorted to do all she could to remove, as fast as possible, the hindrance to her attendance at communion.

Further questions required information regarding the husband, the state of the marital relationship and the relationship with neighbours.

One woman who said she had lost two children was asked what work her husband did. When she said he was a driver, the leader told her that if the children had not died her husband himself would have died; but she should go and get certain named African herbs for her bathwater and she herself, as well as her husband and the coming child would be preserved alive. Another woman was asked whether she had any quarrel with a neighbour regarding the kind of sieve used for cassava flour. She thought for a while and said that, months previously, a woman from another village had left a sieve at her kitchen; she had never used it, as she herself possessed all the sieves she wanted and they were better than the one in question. The leader told her to seek out that woman and return her sieve; she had probably forgotten where she left it, and was now wanting it for use, in any case, as soon as the patient came forward he saw in the spirit that her trouble was somehow connected with a sieve.

The leader ended the questioning of each patient by saying to her: 'Now, let me hear you pray.' As soon as the patient started to pray he would join in, speaking 'with tongues' and most times his assistants, uniformed like himself, would also join in, they praying in the local language. At the end the leader would dip a finger in oil, rub it on the forehead of the patient three times, each time making the sign of the cross, and saying: 'I anoint you in the name of the Father and of the Son and of the Holy Spirit;' finally he pronounced a benediction very similar to that used in the Evangelical Presbyterian liturgy for the baptism of adults.

On a Tuesday. Some patients were gathered in the chapel in little groups, others were in their huts, but all were praying. Each group was being guided by one or more of the leader's assistants, and he himself passed from one group to another, joining them in praying. Apart from the anguished but subdued mutterings audible near the chapel and the huts, a weird calm pervaded the entire settlement till about 4 o'clock pm. I learnt that only short and infrequent pauses were allowed to interrupt the prayers throughout the morning.

On a Wednesday. The chapel was fairly filled by children and their parents, mostly mothers, when the leader arrived, wearing simply his ordinary cloth. He said a cheerful greeting to all, which was eagerly returned in the same spirit. He asked if all the children had been behaving properly, going on errands for their parents, helping their mothers in the garden and the kitchen, etc., and the children shrieked an enthusiastic affirmative for answer. There was a very pleasant general atmosphere, all appearing to be completely at their ease.

A mother whose child would not keep quiet took it out with some show of annoyance. On her return, the leader asked her if she was still angry and said: 'Anger is bad; "the wrath of man does not do the will of God" it leads to hating and that is very bad.' Then, turning to the others he said: 'Have any of you mothers been guilty of anger and hating recently? If so, you must confess it now, so that your children can be helped.'

A woman confessed that she had been very annoyed with her husband. Their child had asked for maize porridge for dinner, and she had used her husband's last remaining four lumps of sugar for it. When he missed his sugar at the time of having his usual drink of coffee before going to bed, she told him about it, but he got excited, saying that he had been saving up those four lumps for his coffee, and asking whether a man could no longer have anything of his own, or whether it was too hard for women now-a days just to walk over to the sellers and buy some sugar. Then he threw the coffee away and went to bed. She was so annoyed that she determined to replace his sugar for him there and then, even if she had to walk to the next village for it; however, when she went out, the streets were very dark and nobody was abroad anymore, so she did not go. On the following morning she felt that she might also have made a mistake.

Several other 'confessions' followed, all more or less similarly delightful in their simplicity, and one wondered whether this was all that the good women had in the way of problems. The leader, using James 5. 9 as his text, warned them against all sorts of bitterness in their homes, as it affected their children's health. The word used in the local language for 'grumbling' (tsedudu) literally represents a characteristic sound made to express a combination of disgust, spite and anger. The leader enlarged on the wickedness of this act, saying that many wives did it behind their husband's back; that Scripture stated plainly how account would be taken of this particular act of tsedudu in the day of judgment, and that it would not be a playing matter then! A hymn was sung, a prayer said, and the children came forward or were brought forward one by one to receive attention.

A woman complained that with the slightest temperature her child would become extremely weak. Asked if she had any quarrel with anyone she replied in the affirmative, saying that it was a serious one. She had been absent when the chief's gong-gong had been beaten summoning people to report for communal service on a certain day; when she was called to explain why she had not turned up, and when was telling the men how she had been at home and knew everything. That was not true. She afterwards quarreled with this other woman in the street, they exchanged very abusive words and even fought a little before they were separated. She was told to make her peace with this woman if here child's health was important to her.

Another woman said her son was a bad boy, and had always been like that; rude, ruffianly, unwilling to help in the house, always only fond of playing with a ball; she wanted God to give him a new character. The leader asked whether she herself had stopped using abusive words when trying to correct the boy; she said that since their last visit she had indeed again slipped once and called him 'big head,' but although she was trying hard the boy's character was making no progress whatsoever. She was told that it would improve when she herself had learnt to control herself and her house as its true mother. (There was a play on words here, as the Ewe word for a married woman literally means 'the house's mother'). The subject of the conversation looked on attentively, and meekly submitted to the subsequent treatment without uttering a sound or giving any other indication of what he was thinking.

A boy, about 12 years old, came forward. He was in school at Kpeve, but was completely unsuccessful in his studies, and wanted help in order 'to be able to understand.' The leader sent him away, saying that the chief elder of the Church in that town had threatened to ex-communicate anyone who came to their group. Then he told me on the side that the boy's father was a prominent member of Tadzewu (which is a rival sect). After a while, however, this boy came back again, accompanied by two women who begged on his behalf for treatment. He was directed to kneel before the leader and to pray. Obviously overpowered with emotion he trembled a little and said, slowly, 'O, dear Father God, please give me also just a little ability to study, have mercy upon me,' then broke into tears and sobbed away, unable to say more. After anointing him with olive oil from the two seashell containers on the table, as he had done in the previous cases also, the leader told him to keep some camphor with him and inhale the smell whenever he could; also to cook the leaves of a certain flowering plant and put the concoction in his bathwater.

A mother said that her child would start up violently upon the slightest sudden touch; it was 'abnormally afraid.' The leader prescribed the inside of an onion, mashed in Everett hair oil, to be used for rubbing the child. For anther child who was said to have a bad spirit, because he was 'tough and destructive' the leader likewise prescribed, after he had exorcised the spirit in a prayer 'in tongues,' cream oil and salt for rubbing.

A student teacher at a Government Training College came with his wife and their twin babies, a boy and a girl. They had been married for a long time without having any children, but after the wife had been to the group for healing she had conceived and given birth to the twins; they had come to present the babies and to express their deep gratitude. They were asked to pray, the man first, on behalf of the baby-boy, and then the woman on behalf of the girl. The leader then warned them against performing any of the pagan rites customary for twins, and told the man he should not refuse any preaching appointments which the minister might ask him to take. As they were leaving he said to me on the side, shaking his head a little: 'That boy, when he grows up, will be a difficult person, and he will once fall down from a coco-nut tree.'

On a Thursday. This being the busiest day of the week at Etodome not only the chapel itself, but also the shed of palm branches erected at its western end, was filled with people. On the raised section near the altar stood 15 men and 18 women assistants, all dressed in spotlessly clean and neatly pressed white long robes, the women also wearing white headkerchiefs or turbans. The women stood on the right side of the altar facing the congregation, while the men stood on the left. When the leader arrived, he was wearing an ornamented red cape over the long white robe which he wore alone on the other days of the week. He announced hymn number 47, which was powerfully rendered, many in the congregation singing all the verses from memory. Then the leader gave a short address on Rev. 22. 15.[8] He dwelt on the distinction between strength of body and strength in the spirit. Those whose sins had been forgiven also obtained healing of the body. Some very strong words were said concerning those to whom the text was said to refer as 'dogs.' Attention was often drawn to the inscription 'Holy, holy, holy is the Lord God of Zebaoth' on the wall above the altar. It was stated that when Our Lord reported back to his Father in heaven after his sojourn upon earth, he used the words 'Veni, vici, vidi' (sic) meaning: 'I went, I did not see him (i.e. Satan), and I conquered.' The Evil One would not stay to do battle with our Lord; he hid himself, but contained to trouble Christians in the world.

The leader appeared nervous and fidgety, and was particularly restless with his hands. He said that he was a mere learner in the things of the Lord, and had only the tongue of a learner. (An odour of sound bath soap which filled the atmosphere was very pleasant indeed). At the conclusion of the address the leader turned towards the east and recited the 90th psalm. Then he knelt down and prayed with outstretched hands, first in the local language and then in 'tongues.' A concluding hymn was sung and then the healings began.

In general they followed the same pattern as on other days: questions and answers on the person's particulars and specific requirements, prayer by the patient which is joined in by the healer, resting his right hand on the patient's head, anointed in the triune name with the benediction that both body and soul should be whole, then dismissal. Several healing groups were formed, the patients being called up in the order of their sitting. It was obvious that practically everybody was trying to avoid going to the assistants, so the leader stopped in the middle of the proceedings and spoke as follows: 'Why do you not wish to go to my colleagues? It is faith that is essential, not coming to me myself. If again I notice someone refusing to go to any of the others in the order, I shall send such a person home. I simply cannot do everything alone. You are yourselves gods if only you have faith. My red dress is no sign that only I can effect cures.'

A slight commotion arose when a woman, who had gone out ostensibly to do something for her baby, suddenly rushed back when she noticed that the next person to be called would be sent to the leader. He rose again and said: 'Please remember that this is the house of God and we are here performing an act of worship. This is not a marketplace or an ordinary hospital clinic. If we cannot behave like those at worship, then we would need to bring the session to an end.' Whereupon there was order once more, the usher insisting that the offending woman should go and sit at the very end of the queue, which punishment seemed to be approved by the rest.

The most striking cases were three for the 'expelling of evil spirits.' A girl of some 17 - 18 years, well dressed and obviously educated and well brought up, came forward. She was to have gone to one of the assistants but the leader motioned for her to be sent to himself. He told me on the side that she was a serious case, and that I should soon see her become possessed. While saying her prayer, she suddenly began to sway backwards and forwards, and soon thereafter started shaking violently, apparently against her own wish. Suddenly she rose up and ran out of the room, shrieking horribly. Several of the assistants hastened out after her, made a ring around her and began to sing, to the rhythm of a tambourine: 'Let the evil spirits depart from the land. May the light reign!' She danced to the music round and round the inside of the circle, looking quite distracted and wild. Time and again she had to be restrained from trying to tear her clothing away; repeatedly the senior assistant tried to put his hand on her head and to say a prayer, but she broke away and would not let him, and it was said that she was not ready as yet.

The leader explained to me that it was the spirit of one of her ancestors, known everywhere around as the most outstanding fetish-priest of his day, which was trying to take up abode in her and use her as a medium. She herself, as an educated girl, her Christian parents and her schoolteacher brother, were all strongly against any such development, but the old man had been a wily one in this life and the case was not yielding easily to treatment. But she still had a half-and-half chance of winning her freedom. I asked what would happen if she were removed to a totally different part of the country, and was told that that in itself would not help her and that the spirit, frustrated in its plans, might even destroy her. The thing to do was therefore to get her covered with the mighty protection of the power of Jesus.[9]

When she had danced and jumped and raved for well over two hours, she lay prostrate and exhausted on the ground, her clothes muddy and in a sorry mess. The leader, surrounded by his assistants, pronounced a long prayer in 'tongues' over her, after which she was carried away. I saw her again that afternoon, normal, very gentle and coy.

The other such cases were not very different, except that in one the girl concerned calmed down much more quickly than in the case described, whereas in the other the boy ran far, far away into the woods, followed by his own people.

[3]

Aside from its healing activity, this movement aims at reform of Christian living within the Evangelical Presbyterian Church. It would remove hypocrisy, disregard of the Church rules, and general lack of zeal in the service of God; it would strengthen the habits of fervent prayer, Bible study, pure living, and good works. Not only the leader himself, but also some of the elders to whom I spoke, stressed the urgent need of such a renewal within the Church at the present time. Hardly anybody would wish to dispute this.

The leader, Mr. Do, is a person whom one might call a saintly character. He is a man of natural yet dignified humility, extremely modest and simple in his way of living; in his religious activities and concerns he gives a convincing impression of great sensitiveness, an intense singleness of purpose, and complete sincerity. He is rather slow in movement and usually of a calm demeanour, but during the performance of a religious act or in a religious discussion his eyes and fingers would become quite restless. About four years ago, his first wife left him to go to another man. He told me that since he began to develop his present interests and activities she had grown more and more dissatisfied with him, often charging that he was 'dull, uninteresting, and not a real man at all.' They had been quite happy together before, and had four children, the oldest of whom, a girl, was about 18 years of age. He spoke kindly of his former wife, saying that her behaviour was due to ignorance of anything in life apart from that which we shared with the animals. He has since married again.

His reaction to something I said illustrates both his openness to new ideas and his confidence in his own light. We were discussing the banning of women who are in their monthly course, from public worship and all participation in group activities, and he had made the point that this was necessary because in that state they were unclean and an abomination according to the Scriptures. I said that I failed to see how this could really be so since the women themselves had nothing to do with it; it did not come from any sin on their part, but was rather the result of God's own thinking and planning when he designed the great and marvellous process by which the human race was preserved from extinction; and everything which God himself had made was very good, according to the Scriptures, and could not properly be labeled unclean and an abomination.

When he had taken in the point he looked flabbergasted, and for several moments appeared so obviously agitated and distressed that I felt almost sorry for having caused so much disturbance of his peace of mind. For a long time he said nothing at all, then he muttered, half speaking to himself, "But in the dream I saw filthy things...," and again fell into silence and meditation. I tried to change the subject but he made no response, appearing to be deep in thought, so I also kept quiet and waited. Finally he suddenly started up, seeming to have regained his composure, and said: 'If I am doing or teaching anything wrong, God will surely tell me. The revelation I have had is that this is an unclean condition, and I must abide by it.'

I would have liked him to tell me more about the speaking with tongues. As he did it so fluently and without the slightest hesitation or stumbling, and could go on for a long time uttering ever new sounds, I would have liked to know how this facility was acquired. However, he did not have much to say. He denied having deliberately learnt or rehearsed it, and said that the words simply came to him by themselves whenever it was necessary for him to pray in this manner.

Mr. Do and his group get along very well together with the local congregation of Evangelical Presbyterian Church, in fact several people are leaders in both organization. On Sundays the group worships with the Church congregation at the latter's chapel whereas before dawn on every first Sunday of a month the congregation holds a prayer service at Todzi, the group's hill-side place of retreat. The local Church agent during the time of my visit, Mr. G. Atikawan, is a man of mature understanding and great circumspection, and was holding down admirably the precarious job of keeping the group within the congregation. The central Church authorities have likewise been very considerate and have refrained from any action that might bring latent conflicts to a head. This is a great improvement upon previous polices, by which any deviating developments were compelled to conforms immediately or be excommunicated.

However, their headaches regarding the movement remain. From all over the Church, persistent and ever more insistent demands have been coming in to Synod for a clear statement as to whether the 'new customs' being practised at Etodome are Christian and good or not: if good, why are they not being taught and practised everywhere else in the Church; if not, why does the Church allow this group to continue in them? The 'new customs' are, of course, the prohibition in Church of all footwear, and of women in their menstrual period; fastings; the practice of divine healing and exorcism; speaking with tongues. Already there is in many local congregations, especially in places not too distant from Etodome, heated controversy about the nature, value and permissibility within the Church, of these practices.

Those who offered opinions on the movement to me and my assistant spoke in general to the effect that the leader was a holy man, and it was necessary that there should be such, to intercede on behalf of the common people and help them in their various needs; that, however, the group was not for ordinary people to join, as its rules were even more difficult, and have to be observed even more strictly, than those of the church.

NOTES

[1] 'And they said to him, "There came a man to meet us, and said to us, 'Go back to the king who sent you, and say to him, Thus says the LORD, Is it because there is no God in Israel that you are sending to inquire of Baalzebub, the god of Ekron? Therefore, you shall not come down from the bed to which you have gone, but shall surely die.' "

[2] In pagan communities widows must have all their hair shaved off with a razor and the head rubbed with palm oil. This is not only to show mourning for the departed husband, but also to protect themselves, as ghosts are believed to be able to pull people away with them to where they are, if they can get hold of their hair.

[3] Reference doubtless to Acts 6

[4] I Cor. 14. 2-3

[5] A local phrase to designate the day on which wages are paid to artisans and labourers.

[6] 'But to all who received him, who believed in his name, he gave power to become children of God; who were born, not of blood nor of the will of the flesh nor of the will of man, but of God.'

[7] 'Do not grumble, brethren, against one another, that you may not be judged; behold, the Judge is standing at the doors.'

[8] 'Outside are the dogs and sorcerers and fornicators and murderers and idolaters, and every one who loves and practices falsehood.'

[9] A remarkable example of this phenomenon of possession of a living person by a spirit (as the author describes it, '...ces cas de dedoublement partial ou entier de la personalité humaine') is described in an article by H.Ph. Junod in Africa for July 1934, vol. VII, 3 p. 270f, entitled "Les Cas de possession et de l'Exorcisme chez les Vandaux.

CHAPTER SEVEN

Other Groups

THE groups of which summary accounts only are given in this chapter, stand on the fringe of our chosen area of investigation in the sense that, while on the one hand they are not products of indigenous Ghanaian prophetism but have been introduced from abroad, yet on the other hand they are not (or are no longer) conducted or supervised by foreign agencies, but are in the hands of local leaders. Two of them need only be mentioned, for the sake of completeness: 1. The First Century Gospel Church introduced from the United States of America about 1920. It flourished for a while but is now in decline, the membership of its Accra congregation being only 66 in 1958; it has had an accession of only 4 new members in two years. There are a few other similarly waning branches elsewhere in the country, but they show no features of particular interest for our present study; 2 a relatively new group, started in 1948, the 'I Am Activity,' also originating in the USA. It gathers some 200 men and women, mostly people in clerical occupations, for study of the literature of the sect imported from America, and for 'spiritual' exercises. It is interesting that this body requires literacy in English as a qualification for membership, the other requirement being attendance at the seven fundamental classes of instruction, on the successful completion of which a member receives a 'testimonial card.'

THE AFRICAN FAITH TABENACLE CONGREGATION

This body is in one place only, namely, Anyinam in the Akim Abuakwa district (postal address: P. O. Box 50). It is housed in an extensive rectangular compound with buildings on three sides. On the two longer sides, facing inward, are rooms which are hired out to patients who go there for healing, whereas the building on the short side provides the private quarters of the proprietor and leader. One of the two sheds in the compound serves as a common kitchen for all, whereas the other, provided with forms, is used for services and 'spiritual prayers.' This accommodation having proved insufficient for the numbers of people coming for healing, a new settlement, called 'New Bethlehem,' has been created at a distance of about 100 yards from the old, on the other side of the main road. This is a much larger area, and has several huts standing on it, with vegetable gardens around them. Here patients may stay conveniently for considerable periods of time.

The Faith Tabernacle connection was first established at Anyinam by an agent sent from Keta about 1919. Mr. James Kwame Nkansah became a foundation member and being a fairly well-to-do local man, placed his own house at the Church's disposal for use as its meeting place. He gradually also took over leadership in all Church's activities, and when the central administration of the Church in Ghana collapsed, Mr. Nkansah assumed full control of the entire establishment, added the word 'African' to the older name of the connection (thus making it the African Faith Tabernacle Congregation), and for himself adopted the title of 'Prophet.' In 1958 Prophet Nkansah, who is also a farmer, was about 73 years old.

Prayers are held every day at 5 am and 7 pm. The prophet then spends his time receiving visitors and holding special sessions of prayer for divine healing. He spends most of the morning in the older house, and most of the afternoon at New Bethlehem. When patients under treatment see him coming, they must kneel on the ground and bow their heads. He places his right hand on them and blesses them. It is said that the majority of those now coming to seek help are pagan cocoa farmers. My informant said that they came not only to be healed but also to obtain accessions of strength or power (Akan: tumi) for themselves personally, as well as for their farms and other undertakings.

They bring such liberal presents that the prophet now owns considerable property. One such present from a chief in Ashanti was a touring car. Also, when the prophet goes on trek, as he does from time to time, he returns with truckloads of all kinds of farm foodstuffs, sheep, goats, and chickens. He owns three big lorries with which he runs a transport business. They bear the motto: 'Onyankopon ye tumfuo' (i.e. 'God is a mighty One') by which they are recognized by adherents of the group, who prefer to use them, and usually send letters and presents by them to the prophet. I was told that some farmers, wishing strongly to offer a present for some special blessing, and having nothing at the time, would even promise a certain portion of their forthcoming crop, which, in due course, is collected. Many give cocoa instead of cash.

Apart from those who come only for healing, there is a core of members of the 'congregation.' A man who spoke to me said that he had been one but had left the group, along with many others, because the prophet had now made everything his own and was more concerned with his own advancement in the world than with the spiritual work itself. The movement is said to have spread from Anyinam to many other places, even as far afield as the French Ivory Coast, and had about 120 local pastors. Admission is by baptism and total immersion in a running stream is the rite used. Male members may come with the number of wives that they have at the time of joining, but they may add no more thereafter. The prophet himself has one wife only, and seven children two of whom are in secondary schools.

If no statistics of branches or membership are kept, there is, however, a whole roomful of files, in which the particulars of individual case histories are recorded. These files as well as biblical mottoes printed on cardboard for distribution to patients as appropriate, are constantly being made by a man at the prophet's house. For all high occasions, particularly the special sessions for divine healing, members male and female, wear long gowns of various colours but all with the same red bands. There is much singing, drumming and dancing on these occasions as the prophet goes round exorcising evil spirits and diseases, or pronouncing blessings. He claims to have cured all sorts of ill-health in this way: blindness, deafness, paralysis, barrenness, insanity, etc. Contrary to the usage of practically all other 'spiritual' leaders in the country, he does not keep any fasts saying that he does not need to fast in order to have spiritual power, and that in fact he has never fasted since taking over his office. However, while fasting is not required in his group, many patients in fact practise it from a belief that it helps in their healing, and he neither prohibits nor even discourages it.

THE ETERNAL SACRED ORDER OF CHERUBIM AND SERAPHIM SOCIETY

A number of distinct groups of various levels of sophistication and without any apparent linkage among themselves, operate under this name. The movement is of Nigerian origin, and is discussed in Dr. Parrinder's Religion in an African City (p. 119f). Perhaps the following comment by this author explains the lack of cohesion among professing members in Ghana also, as noted above. Five churches belong to the central Seraphim organization in Ibadan. But the name has become popular, and societies are springing up, quiet independently, usually in a new part of the town, as a result of a dream or vision in which some new name is revealed.' Whereas Dr. Parrinder gives the founder's name as Moses Tunolashe, both the groups in Ghana which we have seen, called him Moses Orimolade. Both these groups are small ones, each counting hardly more than 100 members.

(a) That which has its centre at a place on the beach at Korle Gonno, Accra, on land kindly placed at their disposal by the Chief of James Town, is headed by a prophet (he is so addressed by the members) by name Adegoke. The centre is only a temporary structure, fenced round with matting of coconut palm branches. The prophet is a Nigerian, his hometown being Oshogbo; he is in his fifties, was formerly a carpenter, and is illiterate. He stated that he used to have eight wives, by whom he had sixteen children altogether, but as many as twelve of them had died. It was this continual loss of his children that brought him into the group. Since becoming a prophet he had dismissed seven of his wives, retaining one only; his remaining four children have remained alive. He trained for six months under the original founder of the society before taking up his present position.

At the death of his twelfth child he was so downcast that he wanted to commit suicide. Two men who were already members of the sect came to him and said that they had been told by the Holy Spirit that he wanted to destroy himself, and that they had been sent to save him. They took him with them to their church. There he was told to fast for seven days, and to pray during that time. In the course of this he once fell unconscious, and saw two angels flying towards him. They took him to a marvellous place which they said was heaven, but told him that since he had not done enough good upon earth he could not be admitted there. He should therefore leave his own family home, and thereafter live in the precincts of the Seraphim church.

One day during prayer and fasting it was revealed to him that he would be sent abroad to do the Society's work. He protested, since he did not know any other language than his native Yoruba. On a later occasion Ghana (then Gold Coast) was specified as his sphere of activity, so he came, and started a branch of the Society. He was, however, entirely on his own, and did not receive either support or direction from his home base. He lived by the casual gifts brought by members, in money and in kind, as thankofferings for healing or other help rendered to them. Collections were taken at services. These he used partly for repairs and maintenance of the house, and partly for the upkeep of the Society's poor sick, who lived there while undergoing healing. Members had failed to respond to his exhortation to them to tithe for the support of the Society.

Anybody can join at any time, and must be baptized by immersion in the sea, whether previously christened by some other body or not. Those who join are nearly always people who are facing special difficulties in life in one way or another: sickness, lack of success in business or any other undertakings, sterility, etc. The prophet 'gives up his own body to suffer hunger on their behalf, so that God may take pity on them and grant their requests.' The severity of the fast depends upon the seriousness of the case.

Often it is necessary for the petitioners to go and live at the Society's premises for a time and, at prayer-time during the fast, to roll in the sand on the ground as a sign of deep sorrow, sincere self-humiliation, and earnest pleading. During the public services all the usual 'spiritual' activities are practised. There are daily prayers at 6 am and 6 pm; a 'vigil' is held at midnight on Saturday, whilst the grand church service of the week takes place from about 10 am to noon on Sundays. Except for the prophet's own white flowing gown, no uniforms are worn. The membership is not stable, many leaving once their immediate objective has been attained. Members are practically all uneducated, and the form of occupation predominating among them is petty-trading.

Adegoke's story of the call to mission of the founding prophet of his group differs from that given by Dr. Parrinder. It is to the effect that Moses had been sick for seven years and could not walk. One night two angels appeared to him and raised him up from his bed of sickness. The angels told him that if he would agree to found a church as specified by them, he would be able to walk again. Although at that time only an illiterate pagan, he knew who angels were and gladly consented to do as they had said. He was immediately cured, and proceeded to honour his part of the bargain.

(b) The chief story of the other Seraphim group, at Kaneshie, Accra (postal address: P O Box 4) is of the miraculous birth of their founding prophet, not of his call. It is said that when he was in his mother's womb, she went one afternoon to a nearby farm to collect firewood. In her condition she could not easily bend down to lift the bundle to her head. Suddenly she heard a voice promising to help her do so, and immediately she found the bundle of firewood gently placed on her head. Later on, the woman realized that it was the child in her own womb who had thus spoken to her and helped her. The child started walking on the very day of his birth.

A certain Ga man, who had spent some time in Nigeria, Stanley Walter Quarmina Botchway, on his return home to Ghana in 1931, started the group here. He died in 1954. The present leader is a lady civil servant, Beatrice Quaye. She is married and has four children, and was in 1958 about 48 years old. She has been a member for five years, and only recently came into her new position by popular vote of her fellow-members. Her robe of office is a long, flowing, loosely-fitting white gown, with long, wide sleeves and a sort of cape, while her title is 'Elder.' In her opinion, the Society should concentrate on fostering brotherhood and good fellowship among its members, and upon doing humanitarian good works to society in general, rather than upon the healing of illnesses.

No non-Christian may be admitted. The method of receiving a new member is by the laying-on of hands, not baptism. Fasts are kept as decided from time to time. Monthly dues of one shilling per person are collected and applied to meeting general expenses. On Fridays religious meetings on the usual 'spiritual' pattern are held from about 5.30 to 7.30 pm; every other Saturday is observed as a day of 'special intercession,' when the same activities are carried on from 10 pm to 5 am on Sunday. For meetings members must wear robes similar to that of the 'Elder,' though not so elaborate; on the fortnightly occasions holy water, incense and candles are profusely used. Members are mostly clerical staff with elementary school education. It was said that of late their number was tending to decline.

(c) There still exists at least one other group which goes under the name of the Sacred Order of cherubim and Seraphim Society, believed to be composed mainly of people with a post-primary education, many of them alleged to be trained teachers and even catechists of the 'historical churches.' But it is strictly a secret society, and information about it is extremely difficult to obtain; I reproduce, as Appendix D, a mimeographed release by the Christian Council regarding them. It will be seen that this is a secret society with esoteric and magical doctrines and practices. Some time ago certain persons, members of the Presbyterian Church at Ada-Foah, were arraigned before a Church court on a charge of belonging to this body. They proved most uncooperative and uncommunicative. The matter had arisen through the fact that they had been conspicuously absent at a communion service held on a Good Friday. All that the man supposed to be their leader would say was that their Society considered it unutterably disgusting for the Church to offer the flesh and the blood of Christ for eating and drinking at the very time when he was still hanging on the cross.

(d) The decline in the number of the Kaneshie group of Seraphim members is doubtless due, at least in part, to the fact that a section of them has split off and formed a new group. The quarrel is said to have been caused by the dictatorial ways of the founder, Quarmina Botchway. The splinter group, claiming to have become at least as large as the original one, calls itself St. Michael's Christian Spiritualist Temple of Light 'Greater World.' Their leader is known as 'Praying Father,' and officially wears a blue gown with white surplice. Apart from these details, however, they have preserved all the aims, customs and ceremonies of the parent body. On a pamphlet which I saw in the hands of one of them was the address: Greater World (Christian Spiritualist League) Sanctuary, 3 Lansdowne Road, Holland Park, London, W. 11, England. I was informed, however, that the group was in no way connected with this or any other body within or outside of Ghana.

THE CHURCH OF THE LORD (ALADURA)

According to Dr. Parrinder's book already cited (page 115), the Nigerian word aladura means 'owners of prayer,' and is loosely used in that country to describe several kinds and denominations of prayer healing churches. This name or title has become familiar in practically all the other West African territories. The Church of the Lord (Aladura) came to Ghana by way of Sierra Leone and Liberia. It appears to be in two sections, one centring in the North Suntresu quarter of Kumasi and maintaining branches at Takoradi and Sekondi-Essikado (possibly elsewhere too), and the other at Korle Gonno, Accra.[1]

Each centre claims to be the headquarters for Ghana, and they do not have any mutual relations. The one, under Prophet Adejobi, looks to Sierra Leone whereas the other, under 'Captain' I. K. E. Sago, has direct contact with the originating body of both at Ogere, Ijebu-Remo, Western Region of Nigeria. It is, in fact, a signatory to the constitution of the entire connection which was adopted at Ogere on 11th December 1955. However, the Accra organization also uses a sort of catechism (or really a book of proof-texts), that was drawn up by 'J. A. Adenuga, BA Dunelm, Dip. Theology, London, 7 Circular Road, Freetown, Sierra Leone.'[2] Both sections of the church are financially self-supporting and administratively independent of the bodies outside the country with which they maintain connections; neither has any fellowship with any other group within Ghana. It is convenient to let them describe their own Church by presenting excerpts of the salient points from their very lengthy and detailed constitution. Although this is doubtless the work of some professional draughtsman, enquiry revealed that the document does in fact represent the actual practice of the church in all important points except that (at least in Ghana) members do not pay the prescribed dues, but only give collections at services, and occasional thankofferings in money or in kind. Another point which may be noted, because it is not mentioned in the constitution, is that persons aspiring to membership are required to know the Lord's Prayer, the Apostle's Creed and the Ten Commandments before they are admitted. Christians going to them from other denominations are accepted without further instruction.

'IN THE NAME OF THE FATHER AND OF THE SON AND OF THE HOLY GHOST. AMEN.

'Whereas ...

'1. In the fullness of time after several years of European Evangelistic career in West Africa, and especially in Nigeria, it has graciously pleased the Almighty Jehovah-God as of old to arouse spiritual consciousness in the hearts of his people here in Nigeria, in that, Ethiopia or Africa shall raise up her own hands unto the Great Jehovah-God under the Spiritual Guide and lead her own indigenous sons.

'2. In the early part of the Semi-jubilee of the Twentieth century in the year of our Lord on those several auspicious days in the periods of the glorious Feasts next hereinafter mentioned, it has also most graciously pleased the Father Almighty at divers times and Seasons to infuse His Holy Spirit into our most beloved, revered and venerable JOSAIAH OLULOWO OSITELU, the Primate and Founder of this organization (hereinafter called "Our said Primate and Founder"), in that he has been appointed in such a serious and mysterious manner to preach good tidings unto the meek, to bind up the broken-hearted, to proclaim spiritual liberty and to fulfil all such other dispensations as were in spirit declared unto our said Primate and Founder ...

'3. It is considered appropriate that a brief history touching upon the inception of an early activity of this sacred organization be hereby epitomized in a chronological order, that is to say:

'i. During the solemn period of the Feast of all Saints, on the 5th of November, one thousand nine hundred and twenty-five, our said Primate and Founder had his call;

'ii. In the solemn period of the Feast of the Holy Trinity and the Celebration of the Feast of Saint Bartholomew, the Apostle, on the 29th day of August, one thousand nine hundred and twenty-eight, the name "The Church of the Lord (Aladura)" was in spirit assigned to the organization:

'iii. In or about the latter part of the Lenten Season on the eighty day of April, one thousand nine hundred and thirty, a promise of the settlement of a "spiritual Jerusalem" was pronounced unto our said Primate and Founder.

'iv. In the solemn Feast also of the Holy Trinity and the celebration of the Feast of St. James, the Apostle, on the 27th day of July 1930, the inaugural meeting of the Church of the Lord (Aladura) was held at Ogere, a district of Ijebu-Remo Western-Region of the Federation of Nigeria.

'v. On that auspicious day, the celebration of the Dedication of our Saviour and Lord Jesus Christ on the 1st day of January 1931, the first church of the organization built at Ogere aforesaid for the worship of true Jehovah-God was dedicated.

'4. The Church of the Lord (Aladura) has now a large and increasing number of converts and members, a full panoply of Ministers and several Churches in Nigeria, in other places in West Africa and or in other parts of the World and has acquired several lands and built several Churches and houses, and shall continue to acquire more landed properties, freehold or leasehold for carrying on its work.

Doctrine

'The Church of the Lord (Aladura) receives and accepts the Holy Scriptures and the interpretation thereof as the basic standard of its Faith, and besides the special Hymn Book of the organization, other Hymn Books, Refrains etc. which conduce to the worthy praise of Jehovah-God shall be permitted for the general use in all Churches under the aegis of this organization along with the Rituals and forms of ceremony which shall from time to time be laid down by the General Assembly. It shall inculcate upon its members the efficacy of faithful prayer for the saving-health of body and soul, the obtaining of all goodness and the weal of mankind in all matters or things temporal as well as spiritual as enjoined by our Lord Jesus Christ, and also accepts baptism (that is to say, by Immersion) upon a confession of faith in our Lord Jesus Christ ...

Membership

'... but any person also who is already a communicant in any other churches recognized by the organization may be admitted a member of any church in the organization ...

Officers

'The officers (Administrative) of the organization shall be: 1. The Most Reverend the Primate of the Church of the Lord (Aladura) and the General Assembly. 2. The Apostles and the Conferences. 3. The Right Reverend the District Bishops and the District Councils. 4. The Venerable Archdeacons. 5. The Senior Prophets and the Prophets. 6. The Evangelists. 7. The Pastors. 8. The Captains and Acting Prophets. 9. The Teachers. 10. The Followers (while in training and temporarily attached to a local Church under a Minister in a District for Parish experience). 11. The church Leaders; and 12. The Male Cross Holders...

The Women Workers

'i. For as much as it has been enjoined unto us in sundry places in the Holy Scriptures concerning the governing principles and the policy of the Church and without allowing any divergence or misinterpretation of such directions, this organization shall vehemently curb irreverence and disorderliness among the women of the church and shall, observe the prohibition of 1 Corinthians: Chapter 14, Verse 34, to cover practically every possible public activity in which women may otherwise take part.

'ii. Subject to the foregoing sub-section, the women workers shall be organized and the scope and the spheres of their activities in the organization or in any local Church thereof shall be fully and clearly defined...

'iv. The Women Workers may be privileged to bear Iron Rods or Wooden Crosses with the Consent and Approval of the Primate but they shall not lead, conduct or perform any Church rites within or without the House of Prayer except there be no male Minister or Leader and in no event shall a Woman Worker notwithstanding her grade be directly or solely put in charge of a local Church in a District...

'...The Council shall have power to frame an annual budget of moneys required for the maintenance, personal emoluments or superannuation funds of the Prelates, Ministers, Assistant Ministers and other Church Workers, including Schools, Colleges and Training Institutes of the Organization; also to make adequate provision for the celebration of the Feast of Tabbieorrah, the Conference and the General Assembly, also to take such steps as they think necessary for the raising, tax collection and allocating of such moneys ...

'...Any question arising on the interpretation of the regulation governing the District Council shall be referred to the Primate and any decision given by him or by any person appointed by him on his behalf shall be final...

...Any question concerning the interpretation of this Constitution shall be referred to the Primate and by him only conclusively decided...

The Primate

'The Most Reverend the Primate of the Organization shall be the constitutional head of all Churches working under the aegis of this Organization. He shall have authority to exercise all the powers of the organization and all other Prelates, Ministers as well as the whole Organization by the Grace of God committed to his charge shall be under his control and shall be bound to conform to his monitions, prohibitions, and instruction with regard to the affairs of the Organization...The first Primate and Founder shall in his capacity as such Founder hold office for life with option exclusively reserved to him of appointing a successor under his writing...but the next primate succeeding him and the subsequent successor or successors to the Primacy shall be elected...

Services

'It is very important that every member of the local churches in the Organization shall attend the Means of Grace regularly, that is to say: Daily Prayers – Fives Times: a. 5.30 am or 6 am being the first hour of the day;

b. 9 am being the third hour of the day; c. 12 noon being the sixth hour of the day; d. 3 pm being the ninth hour of the day; e. 6 pm being the twelfth hour of the day; f. 9 pm being the first watch night; g. 12 midnight being the second watch night; h. 3 am being the third watch night; i. Testimonial service shall be held once on the last Saturday of each calendar month at 6 pm; j. Service on the Mount shall be held on the first Friday of the month or as occasion may require.

'There shall be Vigil Service on Wednesday commencing at 9 pm or at such other time in the evening as circumstances permit. Also Friday in the week shall be regarded as Healing Day. Prayers shall be said in the evening at 6 pm for spiritual and temporal healing...

'...Lighted Candles, Incense burning carried in procession or otherwise and used ceremonially, also ablution as an outward sign, but of an inward sign of cleanliness, bowing down of heads, hallowing the Great Jehovah-God during Prayers observed by Churches in this Organization are lawful ceremonies. All Worshippers, too, shall put off their shoes from their feet during all or any services of the churches in this Organization.

'All Ministers likewise shall observe the Orders, Rites and Ceremonies prescribed by the General Assembly in the Book of Rituals of the Organization as well as in the reading of Holy Scripture and saying Prayers as in Administration of the Sacraments without either diminishing in regard of preaching or in any other respect or adding anything to the matter or form thereof.

'No female members of the Church working under the aegis of this Organization, who shall be after the manner of women, that is to say, observing menstruation, or who have borne a child (if a boy, shall continue in their blood until after thirty-three days, or if a girl, shall continue in their blood until after sixty-six days until the day of their purification shall be fulfilled) shall while in such circumstance enter into the House of Prayer to worship or otherwise; such female members may however attend the services of the church and take their seats in the appropriate place or places provided for them.

'All the Churches working under the aegis of this organization shall, during the Services within or without the House of Prayer, employ all or any sort of musical instruments procurable such as organs, accordions, timbrels, drums, stringed instruments, clapping of hands, high-sounding cymbals whether manufactured by Africans or Europeans.

'No male member who conscious of having had a cohabitation with his wife or with a concubine shall attend, appear and participate in the services of the Churches working under the aegis of this Organization, be it within or without the House of Prayer without first properly washing himself.

'The Organization believes in water-cure, and water shall be consecrated for general purposes and uses during the services of the Church or at any other time or times.

'It is of utmost necessity that Prayer Gowns (as the essential uniform of this Organization) must be worn by both the Ministers and members (male, female and children) at all the Services of the Church be it within or without the House of Prayer.

Marriages

'Since the Organization is purely of indigenous African origin, it shall recognize marriages contracted according to the custom of the country, but it shall accept and inculcate upon its members to contract the Christian Marriages.

'...Children are not at all baptized in the Churches in the Organization, but they are presented and blessed in the Church in the manner prescribed in the rituals of the Organization.

'Children are deemed of riper years and able to answer for themselves when they have attained the age of 18...

'...Services for the Burial of the Dead are not to be conducted in the Churches working under the aegis of this organization. Such services must be held in the House of or residence of the Dead and from thence to the Cemetery for interment...

Tabbieorrah

'The Feast of Tabbieorrah or the Feast of the Tabernacles shall take place at the Ogere Headquarters on the 22nd day of August in each year. It shall be preceded by 13 fast-days, i.e. self-abnegation or abstention from any food consisting of salt, oil fats, sugar, milk, meat, fish, and pepper. Fruits or cereals cooked without salt are much more preferable for the daily breaking of these fasts.

'Many members (males, females and children) of the Weal churches in the Organization in Nigeria or in other places in West Africa or in any other parts of the World who wish to, shall go out of their several towns and countries to Ogere at this time of the year to worship and to sacrifice unto the Lord of hosts.

'The form of ceremony at the Service of this Feast shall be presented by the Primate and the whole proceedings thereat shall be as directed by him...'

At every station there is a 'faith room' attached to the 'House of Prayer.' The patients undergoing healing, and others requiring something to be done for them, go to live until their object is attained, unless they themselves desire to leave earlier. Three-hourly (sometimes even hourly) services of supplication are held for them, on the usual 'spiritual' pattern, and they are encouraged to go to great lengths in the demonstrations. There is rolling and rubbing one's face on the ground, beating oneself, sobbing or crying with lamentations, whirling around till one falls down with dizziness, etc. Also in their public worship this type of activity as part of the 'spiritual' services tends, in this Church, to be notably more intense than in all the other churches of this kind. Special features of the services include the interpretation of members' dreams and visions had before or during the service, the giving out of 'spiritual messages' concerning the personal affairs of some present (both by the leaders and by member to one another), prophesyings of the future, falling into trances. Also, this is the Church which makes the most profuse use of blessed water, for drinking and washing. The 'House of Prayer' is always full of bottles and other receptacles with water which, having been blessed by being thus kept in the sanctuary, people afterwards take away home with them for use.

The ideas of the leader at Takoradi about God and religion may be of interest. Prophet Roland Nwoke Unaebu was born in Nigeria, had spent over ten years in Ghana and had served in the Army. He was illiterate, but knew the usual Christian ascriptions and few psalms by heart, and could write his Army number. His 'faith room' is near Takoradi market, which is in the form of a great circle, with many roads leading into it from all directions. God is like the marketplace, and religions are the roads. All lead to the same centre. God is very simple, and only men without faith make out as if he were difficult to understand. Anything you can think of, God can do for you, if only you have faith. He can even cook your meals for you.

The Accra leader, Mr. Sagoe, was originally a Methodist. He first heard of Aladura through his wife, who advised that they should join in order to be protected from the misfortunes which had been befalling them. They had lost three children through the evil practices of witches. Since they joined, they became free from all misfortunes through the Church's power of prayer. One of his enemies whom he knew well, became blind as the result of the Holy Ghost's vengeance on his (Sagoe's) behalf. He decided not to remain a mere member, but to become a minister, and it was revealed that this would be successful.

'There is another church on the Aladura pattern and with this surname, near the so-called London Market in James Town, Accra. It calls itself The Redeemed Church of Christ Aladura). It is led by Prophet Ajaza, who also runs a school of 110 children and three uncertificated teachers. But the church is very small and displays nothing that has not been already noted.

NOTES

[1] The Rev. H. W. Turner of the Fourah Bay College Department of Theology, Sierra Leone, who is making a special study of this connection in the West African territories, has very kindly supplied the following note:

The one section had branches with full-time ministers at Kumasi, Sunyani, Obuasi, Takoradi-Sekondi, Swedru, Winneba, Koforidua and Accra (Osu) besides agents in over 40 other places, all under the jurisdiction of Apostle Adejobi of Sierra Leone. This dates from 1953.

The other section had 3 or 4 branches in Accra, with Korle-Gonno under Prophet I. K. E. Sagoe as the centre and other branches under ministers at Cape Coast, Komenda, Asamankese and a few places. This section was under the jurisdiction of Apostle Uduwole of Liberia, and also dates back to 1953.

Both these sections recognized the Founder at Ogere in Nigeria as their ultimate head. In November 1959 J. O. Ositelu, the founder, visited Ghana along with the above two Apostles and united the two sections under Apostle Adejobi as a new 'Administrator General,' with Apostle Oduwole, now designated 'Administrator,' as the second in command. This Church is thus now one administrative unit for Ghana, Liberia, and Sierra Leone, with an annual conference in each country in turn.

[2] Mr. H. W. Turner notes that this book of proof-texts is also in general use elsewhere than in Ghana. The author was once a prospective Angelican ordinand.

CHAPTER EIGHT

Conclusion

[1]

No ulterior motives behind secessions
IN the Introduction I tried to show that, however important political motivation might be in the rise of prophetic movements elsewhere in Africa and in the world, in Ghana it has not been a significant interest in political development and seemed anxious to see political changed, this interest did not at any time become a major concern, neither was anything undertaken specifically to further or to realize it.

Again, there is no evidence that anti-European or anti-Western feeling played a role. Secessions have occurred in times of predominantly African control of the 'historical churches' as in those of predominantly European control. Where reversions to African traditional practices have taken place (such as the restoration of taboos on women during their monthly course), the reason has been the authority of the Old Testament rather than the fact that the customs were African.

It is noteworthy, for instances, that in an area of such importance in African life as the burial of the dead, no new ceremonies have been evolved by the seceders, and in practically all cases these groups have simply continued to use the committal rites of their mother-churches. The prima-facie causes of secession (i.e. as given), self-explanatory as they are, appear also to be fully sufficient, by themselves, to produce the effects presented, and there does not seem to be any need to look for further reasons.

Africans and Western-type church organization
It is true that in building up their new structures the prophetic leaders and their helpers, while eclectically borrowing several elements from the

'historical churches' have, on the whole, followed the basic pattern of the organization of African Communities. As compared with the Western pattern this is less hard-and-fast in the application of principles, rules and regulations, of protocol and 'good order,' particularly at assemblies; it centres round the strong personality of its leader, who is its real pivot, though use is made of all sorts of councils as well; above all it gives more scope to individuals to express themselves freely and to indulge their idiosyncrasies. The development of organization in this direction is natural and inevitable since, in any case, there are as yet only a relatively few people who are sufficiently conversant with Western patterns and ways to feel at home in them.

The difference between the two types of organization shows up most clearly, I believe, at tow points, namely in church discipline and in the provision of financial support. Whereas in the one type, discipline in accordance with codes carefully laid down in writing is carried out with a rigidity that borders on legalism, in the other it is all but absent. When asked about their church discipline, all the bodies interrogated stated that they had their regulations. As a rule, however, these are not systematically codified, or even noted down in writing. Rather they consist merely in the prohibitions generally taught within the group, and offences are determined as they arise.

The sanctions for breaking the rules, as given, correspond roughly to those applied in the 'historical churches.' They involve, for the less serious offences, suspension from certain rights and privileges of membership for varying specified periods of time (in some 'spiritual churches' simply 'until repentance'), and for the most serious, or repeated, offences, expulsion from the church. But the 'spiritual churches' have no records of actual examples of the exercise of such discipline, and the few cases remembered suggest that the church authorities were only confirming the action of persons who had deliberately put themselves out of fellowship.

In the matter of financial support, none of the bodies studied levies or receives regular subscriptions, as do the 'historical churches.' Several of them have tried to inculcate tithing, even making it a point of doctrine, but none has been successful in getting its members actually to adopt this mode of church support. In practice, therefore, all these churches have to depend upon irregular voluntary gifts from members, usually made as thankofferings for blessings received or expected; and upon income derived from special occasions such as harvest thanksgiving, 'silver collections'[1] and anniversary celebrations.

The result of this is, of course, that no budgets can be prepared in advance, and workers cannot be paid, or even promised, any fixed salaries.

However, this latter point is much used for propaganda purposes, in the sense that it indicates the workers' self-sacrifice for the Cause and consequently their honesty of purpose, or that it signifies the greatness of their trust in the Lord to provide.

Further comparison with sects abroad

When the Ghana societies are considered alongside similar bodies elsewhere, one cannot help noticing the modesty and sober reasonableness of their claims. It may be that this is due to the country's good fortune in having been spared the excessive political and other pressures to which the people in other parts have been subjected. In any case, no extravagant promises have been made here, e.g. of shiploads of rich consumer goods to arrive for the appropriation and free use of members, or of the latter being able to drive the Europeans into the sea, as such hopes have been held out respectively in the Melanesian cargo cults and in various sects of South, Central and Eastern Africa.

Again no usages have been adopted in Ghana which compare in oddity with some of the practices reported from elsewhere. For example, Balandier [2] tells how he witnessed a most horrible and revolting ritual performed by a sectarian group in the Boko region of the Congo area. The leader of the cult drove long sticks of a tender wood into the graves, right down to the decomposing bodies, then pulled them out and, with the wet earth sticking on, broke and squeezed the sticks, and called upon the devotees each in turn to drink a few drops of the mixture of mud, sap and water which he had thus obtained. A recent travelers in Central Africa [3] reports a sect in which the custom is for the members to attend services armed with basins and pans into which they vomit at the height of the 'spiritual' exercises, this being looked upon as expurgation of sin. Other vagaries can be cited from other parts of the world. No such things happen in Ghana, where prophetism may be said to be entirely free from millenary messianism and its more startling accompaniments. [4]

[2]

Common characteristics of the Ghanaian sects

There can be no doubt that the 'spiritual churches' are being influenced by one another, and a process of levelling up, both in doctrine and in practice, seems to be under way. For example (possibly since the introduction of the Nigerian cults), ever more groups are attaching a religious significance to water, and using it both for ceremonial washing and in healing; [5] fasts and various food taboos are becoming more widespread; the same understanding of biblical passages on such subjects as ritual purity and women is gaining ground on every hand, though in the matter of exegesis, of course, it is not easy to tell how much of what is professed derives from the group's own study of the biblical sources, and how much from hearsay.

There is an easily discernible common tendency to create new communities which should function like kinship groups. In her latest book,[6] Dr. Katesa Schlosser seems to regard this feature as the most significant element in the development of Bantu sectarian groups. She writes in the Introduction: 'In South Africa, the far-reaching dissolution of the old tribal structures through the occupation of the land by Europeans was followed by an interesting phase of the creation, by the Natives, of new social groups. The origin of these new societies lies mainly in the realm of the Christian churches partly because, while Native policy in South Africa did not favour the development of political organizations by Non-whites, it was very tolerant as regards Church matters. Some of the new groups have developed such distinctive cultures of their own and such comprehensively efficient organizations that their members feel themselves to be new tribes.

'A favourable opportunity offers itself here to observe societies founded by Natives in statu nascendi. This is to be welcomed, as anthropology is mostly confronted with finished structures whose evolution belongs to times from which no written records are available.'

This effort to forge new bonds of warm personal and small group relationships is, however, not restricted to the spiritual churches, but can be observed, in various degrees, also in the other voluntary organizations which are now springing up abundantly in Ghana, notably the numerous mutual help societies. Members assist one another not only with services on important family occasions such as funerals and weddings, but also with money or goods for trading, and in other forms of earning a livelihood.

Again, practically all the sects have set their face against the great and steadily growing evil of alcoholism. On this point some groups take a more definite and uncompromising stand than others, but all show a real concern which is not equally evident in all the 'historical churches.' One can only wish them strength to their elbow, as help to stem the mounting tide of drunkenness in the country is indeed urgently needed.

The groups originating in Akan areas are doing much to supplant their matrilineal system of descent reckoning with the patrilineal. This has been ascribed to the influence of Christianity and Islam. Perhaps the stronger connection is with the new appeal of the perpetuation of family surnames. Whereas formerly all Akans used their personal 'given' names as their surname, now the practice is more and more for the name of the (patrilineal) founding father of the clan to be used for this purpose, and great pride is now being taken in 'the name of my fathers.' It must be said to the great credit of these groups that they are trying to secure that within their membership fathers should bear their full share of responsibility for the maintenance and upbringing (including at least elementary school education) of their children of both sexes.

In the same area they are trying, following the example of the 'historical churches,' to alleviate some of the harshnesses which traditional custom imposes upon widows.

One of the most obvious common weaknesses of the 'spiritual churches' is their neglect of theological study. As has been seen, even where some training of their workers is undertaken, it is done only at a very elementary level, and consists mainly in simply imparting, by the 'copy' method or 'learning by doing,' the requisite facility in the various procedures and techniques usually employed by the group concerned. There is a general tendency to exalt blind faith rather than encourage intellectual and spiritual wrestling with religious problems. Accordingly, preaching, on the whole, tries to make up for substance with dramatic effect, often of a rather low order, occasionally not excluding even sheer buffoonery. Sermons show little sign of careful preparation; although many meetings are organized for exhortation and prayer, there is, with one notable exception, no provision for systematic religious instruction; only the usual themes of the evangelistic campaign approach are reiterated with untiring if at times somewhat affected zeal, the same old familiar catchwords and patterned 'challenge' phrases being endlessly repeated. From the way in which the addresses are broken in upon at any point whatsoever (even in the middle of a sentence in which the thought has not yet been fully expressed) to start singing, one would wonder if indeed the words are still being really heard.

All the 'spiritual churches' regard the Old and the New Testaments as equally the Word of God, with identical weight of authority. In fact it is this view of Scripture that leads to the most important differences in practice between them and the 'historical churches.' The first major point of difference is, of course, the permission by all of them, with the sole exception of the Etodome Prayer Group, of the practice of polygamy. It would be reasonable to suppose that this would operate to draw to them many persons who, while involved in this form of marriage and having no intention to abandon it, still wish to become or remain Christians, but find that they are not accepted into the innermost fold of any of the 'historical churches.' Yet this does not appear to be the case. Such people do not, as a rule, join the 'spiritual churches' unless and until-precisely like all other who join-they believe themselves to stand in need of their help. However, this permission of polygamy clearly plays an important part in the case of several workers who have left, or been dismissed from, the service of the 'historical churches' on this score, and have taken up employment with these other bodies.

From the standpoint of the 'spiritual churches' themselves, polygamy is allowed on principle and is not intended as an attraction. In view of the apparent approval of the Old Testament, and in the absence of any definite prescription of plural wives anywhere in the Bible, the teaching of monogamy is considered by these groups (as by many other African Christian) to be based on European usage and custom, with no religious significance whatsoever. Furthermore, monogamy is held responsible for much hypocrisy and (by a great oversimplification) for such social evils as increased prostitution as well as, (though perhaps more justly), for the atomizing of the kinship group, contrary to African concepts of what is should be, and to traditional sensitivities regarding it. It is not generally realized that the evils lamented spring rather from the breakdown of the former sanctions of African society, due to the multiple factors that shape the modern way of living. Only the future will show whether the pattern and ideal of marriage and family based upon monogamy, and its strong points, will come to be better understood and appreciated in these circles.

But although all the groups (with the exception named) allow polygamy, the attitude towards it is not the same throughout. It varies from frank, unqualified and enthusiastic approval to only cautious, almost apologetic acceptance, and an uneasy reticence on the whole matter.

The Musama Disco Christo Church, for example, is not only trying to keep it under control, as has been seen, but also finds it necessary to frame its official statement on it in the following manner: 'We believe that, (as an African Church) polygamy is not a moral sin'. (No. 18 of Appendix B 1; the italics here are mine).

A notable fact is that all the 'spiritual churches' (along with all other sects) are reverting to the old African custom of separating and placing taboos upon women during their menstrual period. This practice, strongly discouraged in the past by the 'historical churches' (being even expressly and strictly forbidden by some), had to a considerable degree, at least in the more sophisticated communities, fallen into disuse. Its present revival is said to be affecting even certain sections of the membership of the 'historical churches' too. Here again Muslim influence may be suspected, but the reason given by the groups themselves is invariably the Old Testament, often said to have been confirmed by various contemporary visions, revelations or other religious experiences.

The adoption of Pauline views assigning to women an inferior place in mixed assemblies and no place at all on deliberative councils, would seem to be a novel departure, which is rather out of step with the general pattern of things in the country at present. But it is fully in line with the thoroughgoing literal Biblicism of the groups concerned, though not all of them wish to be consistent to that extent.

All the groups show a great fondness for uniforms and distinctive bands, badges and various other insignia, a trait which is shared by several societies within the 'historical churches' also.

[3]

An attempt to interpret the phenomenon of sectarianism

When I reflect upon the general direction in which the basic preoccupations and exertions of the 'spiritual churches' seem to be oriented, this Scripture passage keeps coming to my mind: '...you turned to God from idols, to serve a living and true God...' (1Thess. 1.9)

I believe that it aptly describes the greatest positive step which they have taken.

African life, chronically conscious of enfeeblement, of some ill-defined but vicious

anaemia making the blood pulse less vigorously than it ought, and man's total powers just miss their grasp of full vitality, constantly yearns and gropes for health and fitness. The handicaps imposed by an enervating climate, malnutrition, pernicious, blood- and energy-sapping intestinal worms, pestilent insects of all kinds, uncounted legions of microbes inimical to human life, endemic malaria, and still other ills, are not equally felt everywhere, but this awareness of debility may be said to be general. It is by no means alleviated by justifiable fears of external harm that may descend upon a person at any moment (e.g. a snake-bite), or by the ideas held regarding the role of spiritual agencies in human life. In the circumstances it can be little wonder that the basic human aspiration should be to obtain, preserve and increase what has been called 'life-force':[7] potency, vitality, élan; more vigorous, pulsating, prolific life.

It is doubtless an interesting fact that the word in the major Ghanaian languages for curative medicine (Akan-adru; Ewe-atike, amatsi; Ga-tsofa) is also used for the various charms and talismans intended to afford protection from all threats to life, as well as accession of strength. Thus again it cannot be surprising that the healing art should be set squarely within the religious context, or that the fundamental quest of religion itself should be this selfsame 'life-force.' It is the inspiration and objective of all the multifarious activities in which people concern themselves with various divinities, semi-deified ancestors, spirits, demons, witches, fetishes, charms and spells.

The 'spiritual churches' represent a turning away from these traditional resources of supernatural succour in order that help may be sought, for the same purposes, from the God proclaimed in the Christian evangel. As the needs, cravings and hopes remain unchanged, so also the basic ideas regarding the character of the universe, of its forces, their possibilities and the modes of their operation, have been preserved intact. In point of fact, this turning away 'from idols to serve a living and true God' does not appear to be essentially different from the usual practice in African religion hereby a god or fetish which has plainly failed to meet the requirements of its suppliants, is abandoned in order that another one, believed to be more effective, may be embraced. The 'spiritual churches' indeed have a very strong conviction that at long last the passage has been made from error to truth, from the wrong path to the right one, from darkness to light; and that, because this is so, the newly-found resource of helpful power cannot fail.

Thus I see them as engaged in a prodigious struggle to prove the reality of spiritual things in general and of the biblical promises in particular, taking these in a fully literal sense. They are in great earnest; with an intense concentration of all their energies and a glowing desire, they are knocking, so to speak, on the doors of the other-earthly world with the most urgently-felt needs of their followers, and in the keenest possible expectancy are waiting for an answer.

What is the nature of the petitions presented?

The following passage, written concerning Tigari, a syncretistic cult which flourished in Ghana in recent years, is of interest here because it is fully applicable. In practically every respect, to the 'spiritual churches' as well, and gives a very representative list of the petitions which are, in fact, regularly brought forward among them. I would add that in my own experience requirements relating to health and its functions (e.g. fertility) still by far exceed all others. I have already, in the introduction, expressed my views regarding the role of the effects of the 'Western impact:'

> Requests made of Tigari by adherents of the cult are of the same type as the favours asked of the ancestors and the nature deities, except that, because of culture change, more requests are now directed towards economic improvement. The following were heard at a Tigari shrine during a ceremony, and are representative: A school boy was having what he called 'brain trouble' and asked that Tigari help him to think and to succeed in school, as well as bring him good health. A sick man sent a relative to petition that he be made well. A pregnant woman requested assistance in delivering her baby. A traveller asked for

protection on his journey home. A fisherman wanted aid in obtaining a job in Accra unloading freighters. A trader asked for good sales. A woman prayed to Tigari that she might become pregnant. Another sought health for her children. A man asked that the person who had been using evil magic to trouble the mind of his son be restrained. Another requested that Tigari help to change the mind of a particular woman so that she would look on him with favour and marry him.

It is clear that the requests made of Tigari, as of any supernatural power, vary widely; they may be anything that is not contrary to customary law or the mores of the group. However, petitions such as those for aid in school examinations, for promotions, for success in business ventures, for protection against lorry accidents, and for help in obtaining jobs are recent additions, resulting from the impact of Western culture.[8]

It is asserted with great fervour and the utmost confidence that, provided only one has sufficient faith, and further, that one's heart is 'free towards God' (i.e. that one is righteous and is not consciously hiding some sin), these prayers would be granted. During 'witnessing' services there are usually testimonies about jobs found, promotions conferred, all sorts of enterprises crowned with success, estranged couples re-united, diseases healed, etc. In each one of my conversations with leaders of 'spiritual churches' on the subject of the requests made, Mark 9. 23 was quoted: 'If thou canst believe, all things are possible to him that believeth' (with special accent on 'all things'); some were able, as well, to quote other biblical passages with a similar content.

The leader of the Musama Disco Christo Church, for example, never wearies of stressing, in speaking or writing, that 'Christ is not only a God of salvation of the soul but also a Father that is prepared to meet all our needs.' (See the passage quoted at page 4.) All the leaders but one likewise referred to Mark 16. 17 f.[9] and spoke to the effect that they were trying to realize these powers. They all knew this passage by heart. Mr. Do was emphatic that there were ways whereby men could hold direct intercourse with God about their everyday problems and concerns, if only we could discover and use them.

With regard to the health requests in particular, the Gospel stories of our Lord's healing ministry, as well as references in Scripture to the charismatic gift of healing, are taken as fully endorsing the African traditional quest for healing and health in religion, and it is regarded as one of the major signs of the apostasy of the 'historical churches' that they do not practise divine healing. More than once I heard this point explained to the effect that these churches desist from attempting cures for fear that their gross unbelief, of which they themselves are fully aware, would be mercilessly exposed through complete failure.

But if it is taught that faith is the primary requirement for the granting of requests, equal emphasis is also laid upon certain other conditions which too must be fulfilled. The most important is the first of the Ten Commandments, reinforced by the doctrine of a jealous God, which is illustrated by the many passages in Scripture explaining various calamities in the history of Israel as punishments for idolatry. The old pagan African resources of supernatural power, believed to be continuing in full force, are now identified as actively antagonistic to God, ranged as they are on the side of the irreconcilable arch-enemy of God, the Devil or Satan. Whereas in the old religion it was possible, and even the usual practice, to draw upon the aid of several deities or powers at the same time, for the sake of making assurance doubly sure, in the new religion this is regarded as the most serious offence that can possibly be committed. If someone who has appealed to Almighty God for help, further seeks aid from any agency of the opposite camp, that is not only a sign of distrust and disloyalty but also great blasphemy against God, an affront which can only lead to painful consequences for the person concerned, possibly for his entire group as well. Some of the sects condemn the use of drugs and medicines precisely on this score, making out that it indicates a supposition that God's power is insufficient [10] whereas others, taking the view that every good thing comes from God, do not go so far.

Indeed, that by which the founders of the 'spiritual churches' have distinguished themselves in African prophetism is the fact that they were protagonists for the Christian God and champions of his claim as God against the claims of traditional deities. Although their (and their successors') concept of him is not so much that he is God alone, as that he is infinitely greater than all other gods, yet their main concern has always been to ensure that he is worshipped alone and not along with any other god.

This first principle of faith is common to all initiators of the African prophetic movements which have claimed the Christian name. It is doubtless in this sense that, for example, the Musama Disco Christo Church calls itself 'a pure Christian Church.' There is no trace in any of these movements that the tolerant attitude of paganism to heterolatry has been permitted; on the contrary, in practically all cases the founding prophet started on his career by giving strong warnings to his hearers to put away all other worship on pain of severe divine punishment. Prophet Harris of the Ivory Coast and Samuel Opong of Ashanti (nicknamed by the people Tutu-sebe, i.e. 'cast away the fetishes!') are obvious illustrations,

CONCLUSION

because with them this accent remained predominant throughout and did not become overcast, as in many of the others cases, through the accretion of healing interest. But all the others originally likewise made the same point. As generally understood by the people, this may be summed up somewhat as follows: 'Formerly, because you were ignorant, you served the wrong gods; now that you know the true God, clear away all the ineffectiveness and the fraud, to make room for the real thing in religion, namely, the unfailing power of God the King and Lord of all gods. You will be severely punished if you do not obey.' The attempts at wonder-working, particularly miraculous healing, then usually followed in order to substantiate the claim.

Next in importance for achieving successful petition would appear to be the 'spiritual' exercises themselves. They are not merely incidental or of only indifferent significance: they belong to the very essence of the whole matter and, of course, 'spiritual churches' are something distinctive precisely because of them. Members are carefully instructed and trained in the performance of the exercise, and are taught to believe that proficiency in them is indispensable to the attainment of their objects. I understand the adoption and persevering cultivation of these activities as an effort to discover, within the Christian framework, the truly operative techniques of coming into contact with the supernatural.

In pagan religion, of course, human destiny is understood to be controlled by spiritual agencies which determine and award weal or woe, abundance or want, illness or health, continuing life or death. The various human supplications traditionally presented properly go to them, directed by experts who know the recognized procedures for establishing contact. Now how is this done within the Christian context? That is the problem to which the 'spiritual' exercises address themselves. Since Our Lord's own miracles proceeded directly from the power of God within him and were personal to himself, they offer little in the way of usable patterns of method, and other help must be sought.

In the case of healing (everywhere and always the greatest and most pressing demand), naturally recourse is had, in the first instance, to the practices of the early Church, as recorded in the New Testament. But even passages in the Old Testament bearing on ill-health and healing, are most diligently studied for the eagerly-sought guidance. The leading men of all the 'spiritual churches' show familiarity with the scripture passages which appear to have anything at all to say on this matter, be that ever so slight. One of them (leader of the Etodome group) was able to quote from the vernacular Bible, verbatim and without the slightest hesitation, passage after passage of this kind from both Testaments, some of which I had not previously considered as having to do with healing. Then, of course, all the 'spiritual churches' make use of the appurtenances and procedures of healing which are named in the New Testament: handkerchiefs and napkins, the laying on of hands with prayer, anointing with consecrated oil. Along with these, as has been indicated, the use of water in one way or another has become widespread, possibly due mainly to its significance in connection with baptism.

It must be felt that somehow all this is not enough. The source of this feeling is doubtless the simple fact that, results do not quite come up to expectation. In any case, these churches are constantly in pursuit of ever new techniques, and improvements to older ones, with hopes that they will prove more effective than the ones in use. Like all who are eager to increase their own proficiency the leaders of these churches would quite often discuss their problems with, and show a great willingness to learn from, any who they think may know more efficacious methods of prayer-healing than they practise themselves. Aside from the basic 'spiritual' activities, there is practically always something new being introduced: some new fast, or taboo, or rite, or time and manner of praying, or dress, or (in Musama Disco Christo phraseology) 'system.' The search goes on.

These churches do not all indulge in the 'spiritual' exercises in the same degree. To take the five major bodies of Ghanaian origin, it is without doubt of significance that the ones in which these exercises have been least developed are the two with a Presbyterian background (Apostolic Revelation and Etodome), whereas they have found the most intensive use in the three remaining bodies, all with a Methodist background.

It will be remembered that, up till well into the present century, this latter Church regularly used the camp meeting – revivalist method for evangelization and for fostering renewal. Also its general approach to worship considerably stresses emotion. In defence of his refusal to obey his superintendent minister's order to him to stop the 'spiritual' practices the late Jehu Appiah, founder of the Musama Disco Christo Church stated in his History of his Church: 'As the spiritual work started since the coming of the Revered Thomas Birch Freeman to this Gold Coast of ours, it is nothing new.'[11] The divine-healing 'spiritual' techniques par excellence which have been evolved by the Twelve Apostles and the Musama churches in particular, appear to be amalgams of the procedures of the camp meeting – revivalist tradition and a sort of baptized African spirit possession.[12] Spirit possession is, of course, a permanent and familiar feature of African religion to which, from the camp meeting tradition, intense religious emotionalism and the manner of its expression would seem to provide an easy bridge. However that may be, several points of contact between it and the healing techniques actually in use by these churches, may be observed. In both, the state of ecstasy is looked upon as the climax of religious experience; in both it is believed that in this state contact and communication with the spiritual world is achieved and values are received; the practice of exorcism is connected with both; they employ practically identical methods of inducing the desired state, i.e. rhythmic and repetitious music with special forms of dancing, the presence of a sympathetic and expectant crowd (naturally of very moderate educational attainment) and the encouragement, in various ways of emotional abandon.

It must be stated, however, that whereas in pagan spirit possession exercises drugs may be used occasionally to help the would-be ecstatic and, as a rule, alcohol flows freely among the participating witnesses, these two elements are absent in the practice of the 'spiritual churches.'

[4]

Our next question is: *are these phenomena distinctively African?*
It may be profitable, in the first place, to rehearse the peculiar features in question. Here it is convenient to cite a list of the characteristics of 'religious cults' quoted by Professor Herskovits from R. J. Jones:[13]

A leadership that is magnetic to an almost hypnotic degree and virtually dictatorial in its control over the cult devotees.

Frenzied overt emotional expression, such as shouting, running, jumping, screaming, and jerking as a regular feature of the worship services.

Frequent repetition of hymns transformed into jazzy swingtime and accompanied with hand-clapping, tapping of feet and swaying of bodies.

Testimonies given in rapid succession and certifying to the reception of 'miracles,' healings, messages, visions, etc.

Professor Herskovits goes on to report that Jones 'distinguishes groups whose "entire programme seemed designed to magnify the personality of the leader of the cults;" those marked by "spirit possession," a type of highly emotionalized religious and ecstatic experience commonly designated by such terms as "filled with the Holy Ghost," "lost in the spirit," "speaking in tongues," and "rolling;" and those to be considered as "utopian, communal or fraternal"...he essential traits that define them all are, first "spirit-possession" and second the mass hypnotic effect of the group gatherings.'

These observations, though made of American (particularly but not solely Negro) groups, fully apply to the bodies in Ghana, with the addition of such points as the use of indigenous music and special emphasis on healing. But the question remains: What is the origin of such intense emotionalism in religion, and is it something peculiarly African in character?

In the chapter (VII) on 'Africanisms in Religious Life' of his book just referred to, Professor Herskovits devotes considerable space to a discussion of this problem in connection with similar features in much of American religion. 'The problem of derivation referred to concerns American revivalism. Are Negro "shouts" due to the exposure of these people to the white revivalist movement? Or is white revivalism reflex of these Africanisms in Negro behaviour which, in a particular kind of social setting, takes the form of hysteria?' (page 225).

R. J. Jones is quoted a little further on (page 227) as follows: ... the American Negro, as a former slave, received enough of a basic pattern through the observance of white camp meetings to imitate and introduce it, with slight modifications, into his plantation church; ...this was definitely adopted from the whites...' Professor Herskovits describes this opinion as 'the conventional, simplistic explanation of Negro religion.' Apparently his own view is that the religious behaviour patterns in question originated in Africa, were learnt by the whites in their earliest contacts with the slaves, and became perpetuated as a tradition 'which, among Negros, is customarily ascribed to white influence.'

Elsewhere, R. J. Jones is again quoted as writing: '...religious cult behaviour, commonly designated as particularly Negroid, cannot be construed, either in nature or function, in spite of its prevalence, as a racial characteristic' (page 225). And Professor Herskovits himself also has this statement which, though made of Negroes in the United States, is fully corroborated in Ghana too: 'It is to be noted that this summary excepts such denominations as the Catholic, Episcopalian, and Presbyterian, which from an absolute point of view may have no inconsiderable number of Negro communicants, and where the behaviour of negro worshippers, in so far as present data permit any generalization, is indistinguishable from that of their white fellow members...

Similarly, differences between Negroes and whites who belong to these more restrained churches in the minutiae of belief and ritual practices are not known...' (page 213)

Of course Church History abounds with instances of very similar phenomena occurring outside the remotest range of any African influence.[14] It is quite possible that a certain high degree of religious emotion, under a particular set of circumstances, induces certain motor reactions in the human constitution regardless of race;[15] that this phenomenon would occur when and wherever the conditions liable to produce it are fulfilled; and that, if it has occurred frequently enough, a more or less stereotyped pattern of religious experience would develop in connection with it.

Very early in my investigations I came upon a young man who, after praising the virtues of the 'spiritual' exercises to me in the most glowing terms, seemed to me, when the time came, to be somehow unable to give himself up fully to the ecstatic dancing. He was a former member of the Presbyterian Church. At the end of the service I remarked to him that he had performed rather awkwardly, and enquired if he was not feeling quite well. He said that he was quite fit but that, as I knew well myself, his previous church did not teach these things and, not being so accustomed, he always had difficulty in partaking in the exercises, though he knew their value. After that I made it a point, whenever I observed people who seemed inhibited or repressed in the demonstrations, to enquire after their former denomination, and I felt greatly rewarded when it turned out that usually they were indeed ex-Presbyterians, sometimes also ex-Anglicans.

I believe that these are really matters of taste and feeling, and that they belong to the realm of behaviour patterns acquired from the cultural background, associations and upbringing, not to that of racial characteristics, if such there be. Whereas there are Africans who perfectly love the livelier forms of worship, there are others who can only feel at home in the type that has been described as 'distressingly European and dull.' There is no one, static 'African ethos.'

[5]

Local opinions about the 'Spiritual Churches'

It may be stated generally that people do not join the 'spiritual churches' unless they find themselves wanting something or other that the churches are believed to enable them to obtain. Many stay on if their wishes have been realized, or if they are able to continue to hope; many leave again whatever the result of their joining has been. Usually people go for healing after having unsuccessful tried scientific medicine or African herbal treatment or the fetish priest or all three. The 'spiritual churches' are a last resort in much the same way as Christian Science and the like in Western civilized countries. A few said that they went or would go to them because it was a cheap way of getting healed: 'All you need to pay is the collection, and you can make that what you like,'

In our enquires of people living in and around faith-healing centres, about as many denied the happening of miraculous cures as affirmed it. There were those who gave enthusiastic testimonies of such happenings personally experienced or witnessed, as there were those who were only full of scorn, and those who were not sure one way or the other. It was significant, however, that upon further questioning even the skeptics conceded that, in spite of their lack of conviction or even definite disbelief, they might still try any or all of the 'spiritual churches' in time of real need, especially when scientific when medicine had failed. The reason usually given was that in such cases one ought not to rest until all the known sources of help had been exhausted, and even then one ought not to give up because nobody could say what might happen.

Some people offered the opinion that if healing took place it did so entirely on the strength of the patient's own faith alone; others held the view that healing came as a result of the secret use by patients of all sorts of drugs, contrary to the undertakings given to the faith-healers some even went to the extent of alleging that some, at least, of those healers who said that drugs should not be used, themselves secretly used them. The straightforward acceptance of miracle without some form of rationalizing, came far less frequently than I had expected. However, it was not possible for us to attempt more than merely to note these various opinions and attitudes.

[6]

What are the basic differences between
Ghanaian prophetism and Orthodox Christianity?

Practices substantially the same as those of the 'spiritual churches,' have existed (usually within the church) almost since the beginning of Christianity. It is quiet possible even that this religion first attracted popular interest because it was thought to be a healing cult. Reading a book such as Religious Dances in the Christian Church and in Popular Medicine by E. Louis Backman (George Allen and Unwin), one is amazed at the closeness of the similarities displayed. A few lines may be quoted from the summary (ch. 24) of this book: 'Even in pre-Christian times the dance was a means of influencing the invisible powers and of establishing contact with them. This was also the fundamental belief of the Christian church...St Clement of Alexandria described the dance as a part of the inauguration festivals of the Church mysteries. There was a dance of the angels, and the church dance is an imitation of that dance. One wanted thus to display at the end of prayer the physical desire to enter into heaven. According to St. Ambrose the person to be baptized must approach the font dancing...The type of dance varied even in the earliest Church. Frequently there seems to have been a question of round dances, usually with stamping and hopping, but always with clapping of hands and a certain rhythm ... The choreomaniacs of 1374 were by no means an heretical sect ... they were just very sick people who regarded themselves as possessed by devils and were so regarded by others. The Church took care of them and endeavoured by its own methods of devil expulsion to bring them healing. When they are described by the chroniclers as a "sect" this only meant in medieval language that they formed a sort of association. The meaning of "heretic" in a church or religious sense is not part of the meaning of "sect" in medieval speech ... The connection between religion and medicine is of the most intimate kind and finds ample support in the Bible. It is quite natural that such an important act as the religious dance, which imitates a supernatural mystery, must be taken into the service of healing medicine in the expulsion of devils. And just as the early Christians danced at the graves of the martyrs in order to regain health and to move them to drive out the secret cause of their sickness, so also did the dancers in the epidemics....'

However, the 'historical churches' have developed away from performing any acts the inherent virtues of which are believed to secure or induce divine benefits, religious or other; whereas the exertions entailed in the exercises of the 'spiritual churches' are understood to be directed precisely to that end. In fact the old Reformation distinction between 'grace alone' and 'works' (in this context the performance of special rites, ceremonies and ecstatic dancing) is clearly illustrated here. The 'spiritual churches' quite definitely assume the efficacy of various techniques for securing the benefits and blessings which they desire. Thus, if looked at closely, their religion is in essence a very different one from that of the historical churches, though by the common use of the name of Christ the two appear superficially to be the same.

On the question of the types of requests entertained, most ministers of the 'historical churches' would indeed have difficulty in including in their own lists of subjects for prayer, some of the items received by the others. But probably the difference here is merely a matter of culturally conditioned taste and sense of propriety, since both sides in principle acknowledge that God is the final resource of succour for man in all his needs.

The rigid literalism of the 'spiritual churches' in their interpretation of the Bible has already been mentioned. Although there is great variety of opinion within orthodox Christianity on this point, it may be said that the main stream of tradition adopts a freer attitude in biblical interpretation, and exercises criticism with a view to discerning differences of value as between passages and sections in Scripture.

The 'spiritual churches' tend to lean heavily upon miracle to validate the claims of their teaching. While the 'historical churches' (at least in large part) do not reject miracle, they look for such support rather in the truth and intrinsic worth of the teaching itself, as demonstrated by experience.

The question whether the Christian family should be structured on the monogamous or the polygamous pattern of marriage remains a bone of contention.

Finally there is a great gap between the two trends in the range of their respective concerns and interests. The 'spiritual churches,', highly sensitive to the most pressing needs of their people, tend to be restricted in their entire purview by these very needs. In other words, to make use again of a passage already quoted more than once, if 'Christ is not only a God of salvation of the soul but also a Father that is prepared to meet all our needs,' the 'spiritual churches' in actual fact function as if he were only a Father that is prepared to meet all our (this worldly) needs.

The 'historical churches,' taking a wider view of the needs of man, risk seeming irrelevance in that their people are not always keenly aware of some of the need for which they would cater. In their religious scope, they are constantly straining to look beyond earthly life on the assumption that more important than having all its needs met is for a man to be able to say: 'Though I walk through the valley of the shadow of death I shall fear no evil, for Thou art with me.'

NOTES

[1] i.e. no pennies may be given. Such collections are taken at specified times, e.g. the first or the last Sunday in a month, etc.

[2] In Afrique Ambigue (Plon), pp. 239-240.

[3] Dr. Charles W. Forman of Yale Divinity School, USA, (orally reported).

[4] In connection with the general absence of religious excesses it may be interesting to mention a group which meets at Thorpe Lane, Accra. It calls itself 'Commonsense Muslims.' Its leader, a Ghanaian by name Solomon Adjetey Akwetey (by official title 'Commander of the War of God') claims that, while having full fellowship with other Muslims, they bring everything that they believe or do to the bar of common sense!

[5] Dr. Parrinder, Religion in an African City p. 121, has this interesting passage: 'Early in the morning (the old man in charge of the shrine) draws water from the well. It is an African idea that to boil water is to kill the life that is in it, so water must not be filtered or drawn from a tap, but from a well or stream. People come here after daylight to fill bottles of water, to drink or to use in bathing. All ills are thought to be curable in this way, even sterility.' Dr. Katesa Schlosser, Eingeborenenkirchen in Süd- und Süd-west-Afrika, p. 257: 'The only medicine that the believers are allowed to take is holy water...It becomes efficacious through the touch of the prophet Shembe.'

[6] Eingeborenenkirchen in Süd- und Süd-west Afrika, p. 1.

[7] Cf. Parrinder, West African Psychology (Lutterworth), ch. 2.

[8] J.B. Christensen, The Tigari Cult of West Africa (Michigan Academy of Science, Arts and Letters, Vol. 39), pp. 392-3.

[9] 'And these signs will accompany those who believe: in my name they will cast out demons;

they will speak in new tongues; they will pick up serpents, and if they drink any deadly thing, it will not hurt them; they will lay their hands on the sick, and they will recover.'
[10] Cf. with Christian Science teaching: 'Don't mix your medicine with your prayer.'
[11] J. Jehu Appiah, Musama Disco Christo Church History (Fanzaar Press, Koforidua) p. 44. (Written in the Fanti language.)
[12] There are discussions of African spirit possession in: Parrinder, West African Psychology ch. 14; W. Ringwald, Die Religion der Akanstamme (Evang. Missionsverlag, Stuttgart) p. 43 f.; J. H. Nketia, 'Possession Dances in African Societies' (Journal of the International Folk Music Council, vol. 9, 1957); M. J. Field, Search for Security.
[13] M. J. Herskovits, The Myth of the Negro Past (Harper), p. 211.
[14] This subject is most comprehensively treated in R. A. Knox, Enthusiasm (OUP). It is also discussed in F. B. Welbourn, East African Rebels (SCM Press).
[15] For instance, the description of the coming of the 'spirit' upon a person, by Harris of the Ivory Coast (Katesa Schlosser, Propheten in Afrika, p. 246), by the Red Indian Mary Slocum (H. G. Barnett, Indian Shakers, a Messianic Cult of the Pacific Northwest, p. 25), and by John McGee (p. 91) and several others reported in E. T. Clark, The Small Sects in America, are all remarkably similar.

SELECT BIBLIOGRAPHY

BACH, MARCUS *They have found a faith*, Bobbs Merrill

BACKMAN, E. LOUIS *Religious Dances in the Christian Church and in Popular Medicine*, George Allen and Unwin

BALANDIER, G. *Sociologie Actuelle de l'Afrique Noire*, Paris: Presses Universitaires de France

Afrique Ambigue, Plon

Messianisme des Ba-Kongo, Paris: *Encyclopedie Coloniale et Maritime Mensuelle*, vol. I, pp. 216-220

Messianismes et Nationalismes en Afrique Noire, Paris: *Cahiers Internationaux de Sociologie*, Vol. XIV, pp. 41-65

BARBER, B. Acculturation and messianic movements, *American sociological review*, October 1941 pp. 663-688

BARNETT, H. G. *Indian Shakers*, Southern Illinois University Press

BOZZANO, ERNESTO *Uebersinnliche Erscheinungen bei Naturvoelkern*, translated from Italian into German by Dr. Ernst Schneider, Bern: A. Francke Verlag

BRADEN, C. S. *These Also Believe*, USA: Macmillan

BROU, R. *Le Prophetisme dans les Eglises Protestantes Indigenes d'Afrique*, Revue d'Histoire des Missions, VIII ann., nr. 1

BUELL, R. L. *The Native Problem in Africa*, vol. II

CLARK, ELMER T. *The Small Sects in America*, Abingdon-Cokesbury

FIELD, M. J. *Religion and Medicine of the Ga People*

GOODY, JACK 'Anomie in Ashanti?' *Africa*, vol. XXVII, no. 4

HERSKOVITS, M. J. *The Myth of the Negro Past*, Harper

HODGKIN, THOMAS Nationalism in Colonial Afrika, Muller

HOLAS, B. *Sur la Position des Religions Traditionelles dans l'Ouest Africain*, Monde Non-Chrétien, nr 26, pp. 183-192

'*Bref Aperçu sur les Principaux Cultes Syncrétiques de la Basse Côte d'Ivoire*,' *Africa*, vol. XXIV, nr 1

'*En marge de l'Étude d'un Culte Ouest Africain*,' *Monde Non-Chrétien*, nos. 27, 28

HUTTEN, KURT '*Seher, Gruebler, Enthusiasten*,' *Das Buch der Sekten*, Quell Verlag

JOSEPH, G. , *Une Atteinte a l'Animisme chez les populations de la Côte d'Ivoire*,' Paris: *Bulletin du Comité d'Études Historiques et Scientifiques de l'A O F*, pp. 344f. (1916), pp. 497f. (1917)

KNOX, R. A. *Enthusiasm*, O U P

MAIR, L. P. '*Independent Religious Movements in Three Continents*' *Comparative Studies in Society and History*, vol. I, no. 2, The Hague: Mouton

PARRINDER, G. *West African Psychology, Lutterworth Religion in an African City*, O U P

PLATT, W. J. 'From Fetish to Faith,' ch. 5, The Prophet Movement

RINGWALD, W. *Die Religion der Akanstämme und das Problem ihrer Bekehrung*, Stuttgart: Evang. Missionsverlag

'*Westafrikanische Propheten*, Evang. Missionszeitschrift, vol. I, nos 4, 5

SCHLOSSER, KATESA *Propheten in Afrika*, Braunschw: Limbach Verlag *Eingeborenenkirchen in Süd- und Südwest-Afrika*, Muehlau

SHEPPERSON, GEORGE 'The Politics of African Church Separatist Movements in British Central Africa, 1892-1916', *Africa*, vol XXIV, no, 3, pp. 233f.

STOEVESANDT, G. 'The Sect of the Second Adam,' *Africa*, vol. VII, pp. 479f.

SUNDKLER, B. G. M. Bantu Prophets in South Africa, Lutterworth
WARD, BARBARA E. *'Some Observations on Religious Cults in Ashanti,' Africa*, vol. XXVI, pp. 47f.
WELBOURN, F. B. *East African Rebels,* SCM Press

Appendix A

THE TWELVE APOSTLES ORTHODOX CHURCH OF GHANA
DIVINE FAITH HEALING CHURCH

Founded by the Holy Prophet W. Wade Harris
AD 1912   AL 5916
In God is all our trust.

CHARTER
To all and Sundry to whose knowledge
These presents shall come.

Greeting in God everlasting...Know ye that we, the Right Reverend Prophet Michael George and Remnant Office-Bearers of the said Church have upon the petition of members resident or near ... granted unto them, this our Charter constituting and forming them, and we have, accordingly, constituted and erected in our 'Garden' and constitute and erect them to be now and in all time coming a true and regular Branch and Centre of the said Church in our 'Garden' to hold Divine Service and Healing in accordance with the rites of the said Church, under the name and title of Saint......................... No..................................on the roll kept by us of those Charters granted for the practice of our Divine Rites as aforesaid and appoint and ordain all regular Churches and centres of the Twelve Apostles Orthodox Church to hold and respect them as such; and further appoint Prophet..a regular ordained Priest/Priestess to be in charge (subject to transfer or replacement as deemed reasonable by the Presiding Bishop); to collect from the members annually such composition for the support of the Church and also paying from time to time such fees, dues and charges fixed by the mother Church as exigible. Given under the hands and seal of the Right Reverend Prophet and Remnant Office Bearers on this....................... of AD 1957 Al 5961.

....
Chairman Ex: Committee
....
Ex: Committee Member
....
Ex: Committee Member
....   The Right Reverend Prophet:
Prophet   ....
Ex: Committee Member   Presiding Bishop
....
   Prophet
   Treasurer
....
   Diocesan Secretary

N. B. – For origin and history of the Church read Arthur E. Southons's *More King's Servants* pp. 96 f.

Note: The Charter is the only printed document available from the Church of the Twelve Apostles. In a letter to me, Mr. Benn explains about the letters 'AL' as follows: 'Ancient

APPENDIX

Religion begins its era with the creation of the world, calling it Anno Lucis (Latin), this abbreviated "AL" meaning "In the year of Light." This is calculated by adding 4003 years to the year of Christ's birth...'(The figures indicate that possibly the number to be added is really 4004.)

Appendix B (I)

SUMMARY OF WHAT MDC CHURCH BELIEVES AND TEACHES

1. We believe only in the Holy Bible and all its teachings as teachings from God. Eccles. 12. 13; Ex. 34. 27; Luke 4. 21; Ps. 119. 105; Heb. 1. 1-2; Heb. 4. 12; II Tim. 3. 15; John 5. 39; II Peter 1. 21; Ex. 20. 3. 17; Matt 4.4.
2. We believe in the Holy Trinity as God the Father, the Son and the Holy Ghost. Matt.28. 19; John 17. 5; Col. 2. 9.
3. We believe in the Divine Birth of Christ. Luke 1. 35; Matt. 1. 23.
4. We believe in the Resurrection of Christ. Rom. 8. 34; John 11. 25; Matt. 16. 21; Acts 26. 22-23.
5. We believe in the salvation of the soul through Christ. Rom. 5. 8; John 20. 31; John 3. 16; Rom. 4. 25.
6. We believe in the second coming of Christ or the Judgment Day. Ps. 50.3-4; Dan. 12. 2; Acts 10. 42; Matt. 24. 40-44; Acts 1. 10-11; John 14. 3; Eccles. 12. 14; II Cor. 5. 10; I Thess. 4. 15-17; Rev. 20. 11-15.
7. We believe that the Holy Spirit can declare his presence emotionally or solemnly. Heb.6. 4-6; Acts 15.8; Rom. 8. 9-15; John 14. 16-17, 26; Acts 19. 1-7; John 16. 8, 13-14; Acts 2. 1-4, 17, 39; Luke 24. 49; Acts 10. 44-48; Heb.13. 8; John 4. 23-24.
8. We believe in all other Christian Churches. Acts 20. 28; Eph. 1. 22-23; I John 4. 1-3; II Cor. 11. 2; I Cor. 12. 13.
9. We believe in confession and forgiveness of sins. I John 1. 9; Luke 8. 37; II Cor. 7. 10; I Thess. 5. 23; Rom. 6 14, 22.
10. We believe in the importance of the Holy Communion (Sacrament) in the Christian life. I Cor. 11 26-28; Matt. 26. 26-28; I Cor. 10. 16-17.
11. We believe in the Holy Baptism in any form. Matt. 3. 16; Matt. 28. 19; Acts 8. 36-38; Acts 2. 38; Acts 10. 47; Col. 2.12
12. We believe in the Resurrection of the body or life hereafter. John 5. 28-29; I Cor. 15. 54; Rom. 8. 11.
13 We believe in Divine Healing. James 5. 14-15; Isaiah 53. 4-5; Luke 9. 2; Luke 8. 43; Matt. 15. 28; Matt. 10. 8; II Kings 4. 24-25; 5. 10-17; Deut. 32. 39; Ex. 15 26; I Sam. 1. 11-20; Mark 16. 15-18.
14. We believe in the existence of Heaven and Hell. Matt. 25. 46; I Cor. 15. 24-28; Matt. 18. 10; 1 Peter 1. 4; Rev. 20. 11-14; II Peter 2. 4: Ps. 9. 17; Luke 16. 24; Rev. 14. 10f; Mark 9. 43-44.
15. We believe in Drumming and Religious Singing as part of Christian worship. Ps. 150. Ps. 149. 3; Ps. 81. 2-4; Eph. 5. 19.
16. We believe in Tithes and Offerings. I Cor. 9. 14; I Cor. 16. 2; Mal. 8. 10; Acts 20. 35; Ps. 50. 14, 23.
17. We believe in fasting and prayers. Matt. 17. 20-21; I Cor. 7. 5; II Cor. 6. 5; Matt. 6. 16; II Cor. 11. 27.
18. We believe that (as an African Church) polygamy is not a moral sin. I Cor. 7. 28, 36; Matt. 22. 30; Gen. 16. 2-3; II Sam. 12. 8; Heb. 13. 4; I Cor. 7. 7-9; Matt. 19. 10-11.
19. We believe that a Christian should be a useful citizen to his country. I Peter 2. 13-15, 17; I Tim. 2. 1-2; Matt. 22. 21.
20. We believe in total temperance in Christian life. Gal. 5. 22-23; II Cor. 2 17; I Cor. 6. 19-20; I Thess. 5. 22; Heb. 12. 14-16; Isaiah 65. 4; I Cor. 3. 16-17; Amos 6. 6; Heb. 2. 15; Isa. 5.11-22.

APPENDIX

21. We believe that Sunday is a Christian Sabbath. John 20. 19, 26; Acts 20. 7; I Cor. 16. 2; Col. 2. 14-16.
22. We believe that Christ is the only Intercessor. I Cor. 6. 6; John. 16.13; John 14. 6, 17; Rom. 8. 9; Heb. 8. 10; Rom. 8. 27; I Tim. 2.5.
23. We believe in a Christian's effort to trample down idolatry, occultism, fetishism, jujuism, spiritualism, secret orders and all other sorts of superstitions. II Cor. 6. 14-16; John 17. 14-15; I Tim. 4. 1-3; Deut. 18. 11; Lev. 19. 31; 20. 6; Luke 10. 19; Col. 2.8.
24. We believe that it is unclean to enter the Temple with Sandals etc. Ex. 3. 5; Josh. 5. 15.

Appendix B (2)
(Sample of Yearly Prophecies)

EVENTS OF THE YEAR – 1959
(Condensed)
(As prophesied by the Prophet M. M. Jehu-Appiah, Akaboha II).

In the name of the Father, the Son and the Holy Ghost, may peace be unto you. Amen.

Businessmen will know this year as a year of much work and little earning. This year on the other hand determines the economic welfare of the following year (1960). As the Spirit declares, you can 'purchase' the future with the effort of this year. The high cost of living will still stand high. It is a year of need while in plenty.

Pious and devout people will notice some 'miracle of Providence' in their affairs of life.

The world war that seems to threaten started about three years ago in the spirit as I prophesied to you long ago. This cannot disturb the peace of this particular year. Though there will be some civil disorder and commotions but these will rather tend to 'preserve' the common peace of the world as a whole.

In this year, there will be many indecent marriages and more divorces as wickedly planned by the devils; so people should guard themselves against these.

As prophesied for last year, international affairs will continue still in this year also and signs of its good benefits will reveal themselves in the fifth and the eleventh months of the year.

Professional men will still desire (as prophesied for last year) to have second source of income. This ideal is much recommended and the 'fruits' of this will 'ripe' from the preceding year, if all things are done properly to the glory of God.

Farmers are advised to make their food farms a week later than last year. January 2nd should be observed quietly with fasting prayers for God's blessings and guidance through the year. Reading of Psalm 1 is recommended after the prayers.

There will be spiritual 'stock-taking' from 17th to 23rd of June. This week should therefore be spent in prayer for God's grace and a day from this week should be chosen for fasting prayers. Also all homes should be kept clean and tidy that week.

The Guardian Angel for the year is Mariel meaning 'Balance.'

He will offer helping hand to them that will help themselves.

Suitable hours for prayers this year is 7.00 am, 11.00 am and 3.00 pm (GMT)

May Peace Be Unto you. Amen.
(Sgd) M. M. Jehu-Appiah.

Appendix B (3)
MDCC Prayer of Cleansing before Divine Healing
(From the Fanti Prayer Book)

'Washing with water or self-cleansing.

While holding up your water-kettle with the right hand, lift up your eyes to heaven and say the following prayer:

"In the name of the Father and of the Son and of the Holy Spirit, Amen. Good Lord, who through water and the Holy Spirit caused the children of men to be born again for a life that is without end, since my parents brought me forth in sin, I beseech thee to make this water wash and cleanse me thoroughly through Thy Holy Spirit, in the name of Jesus Christ, Amen."

After this, use the following prayer while cleaning every part of your body:

"Lamb of God that takest away the sins of the world, I beseech thee to wash my ....from all bodily defect, as thou didst wash thy twelve disciples."'

Appendix B (4)

The MDCC's summary account of itself, taken from its Calendar for 1959:

'COME AND SEE'
John 1. 46.

Can there any good thing come out of Nazareth?
  Come and see
Can I find Christ in Musama Disco Christo Church?
  Come and see
Is Christ prepared to meet my personal needs there?
  Come and see
Can I also find salvation to my soul?
  Come and see
Is the faith of miracles possible in this present world?
  Come and see
Does there exist the miracle of answered prayer?
  Come and see
Can a Christian find help in God at all?
  Come and see
Does the MDC Church distinguish itself from the other independent Churches?
  Come and see
Is the Church recognized by some overseas Mission?
  Come and see
Is the Church registered by the Ghana Government?
  Come and see
Does the Church hold about 20,000 members?
  Come and see
Can the Church extend its services to me while I am not a member?
  Come and see
If I come to Mazano near Gomoa Eshiem can I be convinced?
  Come and see
Christ freely extends his loving hand to relieve you of your burden.
  So come and see

Akaboha II
Musama Disco Christo Church
Mazano,
Nr. Gomoa Eshiem
via Swedru.

Telephone No. 3

APPENDIX

FACTS AND FIGURES FOR 1958

Number of Pastors	30
Number of Catechists and Healers	94
Number of Stations	90
Number of Sub-stations	101
Total Membership	19,800
Total Patients Received	4,716
Total Patients Healed	4,209
Lapses	396
Deaths	109

Appendix C (I)

THE CATECHISM OF THE APOSTOLIC REVELATION SOCIETY

1. *What are the first seven essentials of the anointment?*
   The first seven essentials of the anointment are: -
   1. That I should completely surrender myself to the Holy Spirit and inherit the Holy Spirit as my only real wealth.
   2. That I should voluntarily do all righteous services as a faithful follower of Christ, so that through my sacrifices and kind actions, I should always be counted as His.
   3. That the whole armour of God should be my shield throughout my life's journey.
   4. That I should always speak the truth, endure with courage all tribulations and stand fast in my jealousy for the Lord.
   5. That I should be submissive to all heads of governments, friends and brethren; and that I should be humble, kind, merciful and forgiving as an elect of Christ.
   6. That I should confess my sins always and be penitent in order to warrant forgiveness and I should also forgive my trespassers.
   7. That I should strictly observe all Sundays and Christian festivals, and differentiate between clean and unclean foods.

2. *What are the aims and the seven duties of the society?*
The aims and the seven duties of the Society are: -
   1. That the Society should make known the supreme power of God by means of its work, miracles and signs and to enlighten the benighted.
   2. That the Society should teach the blessing in being merciful so that the members should be merciful one towards another.
   3. That the Society should gather all the scattered flocks under their leader and feeder, Isa. 11. 6-9; that the differences within the Christian Churches be removed; that all should acknowledge the Lord as their father and mother whereby the habits of spite and mockery, consultation of demons and familiar spirits which is commonplace amongst the unsteadfast Christians who have not received the Holy Spirit, should be uprooted so that men should inherit the kingdom of God. Matt. 6.10.
   4. That all which we have neglected should be recovered and the spirit of self-sacrifice be appreciated.
   5. That the Society should remind the world of the second coming of Christ and that awful day of judgment through its preaching of repentance to the children of the world and that the Society should be a fresh inspiration to tired Christians and an awakening to the sleeping.
   6. That the Society by its zeal and sword persecute the unrighteous. Luke 11. 50 and 51.
   7. That the Society by means of signs and miracles should destroy fetishism and its wicked practices so that people could offer their soul and bodies for the building up of the kingdom of God wherein all should honour God the Father, the Son and the Holy Ghost by their actions.

3. *What are the benefits of the outdooring of children?*
The benefits of the outdooring of children are: -
   1. That the children should acknowledge God as their Father and Creator from their infancy, in the same way as they recognize their mother, and adhere to Him by doing His will.
   2. That they should be under the full care and protection of God; for our Lord Jesus Christ said that whosoever shall offend any child placed in His care shall not go unpunished.

3. That the parents of the children should be redeemed from the fear of those who can kill the body, the destruction of invisible evil spirits and undue worries.
4. *What is the Apostolic Revelation society?*
   The Apostolic Revelation Society is a prophetic institution established by Wovenu, an elect of God, for preparing the souls of the people through anointment for death or eternal life in the second coming of Christ.
5. *What is anointing the sick?*
   1. Anointing the sick is surrendering the sick to God in prayer after confession of sins as advised by the apostle James that should any be sick amongst you, he should call for the Church to pray for him and anoint him in the name of the Lord. James 5.14.
   2. Anointing the sick strengthens him in his agony of death so that his sorrows turn to joy. The anointment invokes the hand and the healing Spirit of God to intercede for him with groanings which cannot be uttered and delivers his soul from the pangs of death. Ps. 107. 20
6. *What is marriage?*
   1. Marriage is a divine institution and a divine obligation for mankind to fulfil.
   2. Marriage is a shady tree of God under which mankind increases and multiples.
   3. Marriage brings about the union of man and women and the joy and the help desired one of the other and, ends all the gloom of loneliness.
7. *What is the Holy Communion?*
   1 The Holy Communion is an act of remembrance of God and His Son Jesus Christ who instituted it. It is an expression of true love towards our neighbour which is the will of God.
   2 The partaking of the Holy Communion is a complete surrender of our will to the Holy Trinity and serves as a measuring rod whereby our body and soul are measured.
   3 The Holy Communion unites man and God and the soul and the body. It strengthens us in our repentance from those sins which we confess before partaking of it and it makes us free as we emerge from the anger of God.
   4 The Holy Communion keeps us vigilant (watchful) against all uncleanliness and keeps us holy through our constant partaking of it. Therefore Paul, the apostle, said that should anyone not examine himself properly before partaking of it, he does so unto his own condemnation. 1 Cor. 11. 28 f.
8. *What are Sacraments?*
   Sacraments are divine performances in the Christian Church to render the members Christians and it is a mark of honour which all children of God do deserve.
9. *Why need we know about the Sacraments?*
   We need know about the Sacraments and remember them so as to abide by them. It is a knowledge that builds us and lets our face shine in the light of the word of God. Dan.12. 3.
10. *What is the Worship of God?*
    The worship of God is faith in Him who has created the world and all that therein is. It is keeping to His laws and wishes.
11. *What is the Kingdom of Heaven?*
    The Kingdom of Heaven is the next life preserved by God himself for the inheritance of those who would do His will on earth. It is a place where the souls shall find a great comfort, joy and complete rest and where they will live for ever in the presence of God and His servants.
12. *Who are the Unbelievers?*
    The unbelievers are all those who despise the living God, His laws, wishes, worships and

all righteousness and cling steadfastly to the world and all man-made institutions and worship.

13. *What is Hell?*
Hell is a place of great suffering where God Himself will cast the many that He created but they would not do His will. It is a place where the souls will experience a great discomfort from day to day and their everlasting reward will be a fire, the coals and flames of which never quench.

14. *What are the status and qualifications of Wovenu in the Society?*
Wovenu's status and qualifications are: -
   1. He is the Founder of the Apostolic Revelation Society.
   2. He is the Principal Teacher of the Apostolic Revelation Society.
   3. He is Prophet of God the Most High.
   4. His is Doctor of the Word. (N.B. The Ewe word means 'Physician' not 'Teacher.')
   5. He is the Leading Light. (Lit. 'The King of Light.')
   6. He is the Heavenly key of the Apostolic Revelation Society.
   7. He is Performer of the Sacraments of the Apostolic Revelation Society.

15. (a). *What is Prophecy?*
Prophecy is the voice or message received from God and it is divine gift to those who receive the voices or messages.

(b). *What is Prophecy to the Prophet and to him for whom the voice or message is received?*
Prophecy is only divine duty imposed on the prophet but, it is a great benefit and advancement to him for whom the voice or message is received.

(c). *What ought he who is placing his request to God through Prophets to do?*
He who is placing his request to God through prophets should pray to God always in secret so as to receive his reply from God through the prophets. For, the apostle Peter said that prophecy does not come out of the will of men but prophets speak when they are moved by the Holy Spirit. 11 Peter 1. 21.

(d). *Does God speak to everyone who is asking something from Him?*
Yes, God speaks to everyone, but He listens not to those who are disobedient to His will. It is therefore necessary that if a man is anxious to receive replies from the Lord through visioners, he should be in union with God by way of confessing his sins and becoming penitent.

(e). *Does God reveal everything to his Prophets?*
No. God conceals many things from His prophets in divers ways. For example (a) if the seeker does not confess his sins which he had committed. (b). If what the seeker needs is not necessary, God keeps silence. And so it is a curse to prophets if they are in haste to receive reply and to prophecy at all times.

(f). *Is it necessary that Prophets tell or reveal visions or voices insufficiently understood by them?*
No. If a prophet sees a vision or receives a message which is proverbial or is in a language unknown to him or misunderstood by him, he should be silent till the meaning is revealed to him.

16. (a). *What are alms?*
Alms are sacrifices, thankofferings and honour to God which make us progress, increase our blessings and drive away all evil from us.

(b). *How should we offer alms to men of God?*
Almsgiving to men of God is almsgiving to God Himself which brings blessing to the giver as taught by our Lord Jesus Christ in St. Matt. 10. 42 that whosoever would give a cup of water to any of his servants would surely receive his reward.

(c). *How should we offer alms to men of God?*
As offering of alms to men of God is as good as offering alms to God Himself, we should always offer such alms with clear hearts by way of doing God's will; and secondly, our hearts should clearly be disposed towards the person to whom the gift is made so that our alms may be acceptable unto God. For the scripture says that obedience is better than sacrifice and to listen is better than the fat of rams.

(d). *How many kinds of almsgiving are there?*
There are two kinds of offerings that are good. They are (1) Private Almsgiving (2) Public almsgiving. God is the rewarder of these two kinds of almsgiving as He is the receiver of the alms.

(e). *Should we boast of the alms we offer the men of God?*
As almsgiving to these men is almsgiving to God, it is vain to boast of such action as if we are conferring benefits to them personally, and so we should not expect a reward from them in any form or shape. Further, we ought to realize that whatever alms we offer were first offered to us as alms by God as He is the author of all good things.

(f). *Does God receive the alms we offer other people too?*
Yes. All alms are received by God and He regards this as an act of kindness and counts it as righteousness unto us.

(g). *Is almsgiving to those who cannot return thanks in kind or rewards also pleasing to God?*
Yes. Almsgiving to the poor, the orphans, the widows, the lame and the helpless are pleasing to God. For our Lord Jesus Christ said that He who rewards on behalf of those people is Jehovah Zebaoth, God who is their father and best guardian.

(h). *Which almsgiving please God?*
Small and great almsgivings are pleasing to God. He who has little or much should give according to his worth. Further, almsgivings which comes from our heart without grudge are pleasing to God.

17. *What is baptism or repentance?*
Baptism is a mark of redemption administered by means of water to those who have been Christians. There are two forms of baptism. The first form is the one in which water is sprinkled on the person as a sign or mark of his redemption in the name of the Holy Trinity. This form is best suitable for babies, children and those who are wearied through ill-health. The second form is that in which the person is immersed into water as an ablution mark of redemption. It is suitable for grown-ups. These two forms are good as they are outward and visible signs administered on the redeemed to cleanse them and make them worthy followers of God as is accorded the disobedient and wicked children of God. For, the Lord Jehovah is merciful towards those who love him and keep his commandments. Ex. 20.6.

18. *The Vows of those who should be baptized?*
I would denounce Satan, the enemy, and all his ways and would follow God the great Creator of the world so as to be the follower of His son Jesus Christ and the Holy Spirit throughout my life. I vow to make known the living God and His righteous ways to all transgressors and I would not be overcome by evil. And so help me O! God the Father, the Son and the Holy Ghost. Amen

19. *What are the Ten Commandments?*

1. The Ten Commandments are: -
2. Thou shalt have no other God except Jehovah
3. Thou shalt have no graven image for thyself
4. Thou shalt not call the name of Jehovah thy God in vain.
5. Thou shalt remember the Sabbath and keep it holy
6. Thou shalt honour thy father and thy mother so that thy life should be long on the land Jehovah thy God shall give thee.
7. Thou shalt not kill
8. Thou shalt not commit adultery
9. Thou shalt not steal
10. Thou shalt not bear false witness against thy neighbour.
11. Thou shalt not covet anything which is thy neighbour's.

20. *The confession of faith of the Apostolic Revelation Society?*
I believe in God the great Father who created the heaven and the earth. I believe in his Son Jesus Christ whom He sent into the world and He ascended again unto Him, I believe in the Holy Ghost, God's own spirit of Truth, Comforter and Advocate. I believe in every Christian Church which is an assembly of holy men and the society of those who denounce Satan the enemy and his deceitful ways to worship Jehovah alone. Amen.
(N. B. For the Lord's Prayer the orthodox version is used)

21. *What is giving the tithe?*
   1. Giving the tithe is thanksgiving to God, honouring him and obeying His holy will as is written by the prophet Malachi in Mal. 3. 7-10
   2. Giving the tithe is seeking eternal increase for the few things possessed by one's self both on earth and in heaven.
   3. Giving the tithe drives away all evil from man. It is the surrendering of one's work and possessions to the protection of God and His holy servants (angels).
   4. Giving the tithe brings great blessing, long life, prosperity and self-consciousness. Gen. 12.2f; Deut. 28. 11-13.

22. *What is the best form of following Christ?*
The best form of following Christ is that I should adhere to the divine laws and precepts of God, do the works of the Lord as His servant in accordance with the words of Christ in St. John 14. 12 that whosoever believeth in Him shall do all that He did and greater works than He did shall the person do as the scriptures confirmed in James 2.17 that faith in Christ without work is dead.

23. *Which church is the divine one of Christ and the abiding in its fellowship?*
The Christian church which is divine and pleasing to God is every church in which God alone is worshipped and His laws are strictly adhered to. For Christ said 'Not everyone that saith unto me Lord, Lord, shall enter into the kingdom of heaven, but he that doeth the will of my Father which is in heaven.' Matt. 7. 21. For this cause, the apostles with one accord in the confession of their Faith or their Creed declared to their Lord and God that it is only in that holy church they believed.

24. *Is this holy church established at any one particular place?*
Never: This holy church is everywhere or it is every assembly of people which adheres to the laws and the precepts of the only one God and denounces Satan and his wicked ways.

25. Prayer and fasting.
   1. The essential duties of the initiate of the Society are prayer and fasting. If the initiate is independent, he should pray at least three times a day and three times at night. The hours of his nightly prayers should be 9 pm; 12 pm and 3 am, and the hours of his daily prayers

should be 5 am; 9 am; 12 pm; and 6 pm. But prayers at these prescribed times should not be considered as law. Other hours of the day or night are also good for prayers as the ears of the Lord are opened always. What is only important is constant prayer, for prayer is talking with God. Constant talking to God brings to life, joy and security. It expels worry and fear and we are rendered confident.

2. It is a good habit to fast frequently in remembrance of God so that we should be holy and confident. For, refraining from eating is penance to enable us to draw nearer to God or that God may have mercy upon us. Above all, fasting without eating shows our sincerity which carries our prayer to the Lord. And it is a fact that the Lord listens more readily to our prayer whilst fasting. Fasting is a process of retreat from the world to things divine or heavenly.

3. Fasting coupled with righteous service quickly brings victory. If a person is fasting he should remember not to violate or break the commandments of God. He should not quarrel, abuse, slander, be angry, be deceitful, be treacherous, be greedy or cause anyone to suffer pain. He should be righteous. There are unrighteous ways of fasting as fasting in sin by stealing, drinking, quarrelling, being deceitful, cruel and committing other unrighteous acts whilst fasting. These merely fast to keep their stomachs empty in preparation for a good meal. The Lord does not suffer such people.

Appendix C (2)

PROPHET WOVENU'S SUMMARY STATEMENT OF THE OBJECTIVES OF HIS MOVEMENT

No. 23 of the Ewe Catechism: Which holy tasks did Wovenu institute?
1. The prophet Wovenu instituted the preaching of repentance in his Church, and gave permission for the carrying out of Baptism, the receiving of the Holy Spirit, Holy Unction and Holy Communion.
2. The prophet Wovenu instituted the task of keeping a place for the healing of the sick within the Church, as Christ commanded the Apostles, Mark 15. 17f.
3. The prophet Wovenu instituted the task of caring for orphans, widows, the poor and homeless within the church, in addition to other works of mercy and of kindness, according to the word of God. James 1. 27.
4. Wovenu established fasting and frequent prayers in the Church for the furtherance of these tasks, as Christ said. Matt. 7. 7.
5. Wovenu started town-improvement activities, repair of roads, works of righteousness, and everything that is good for men, as tasks of the Church in addition to literacy and the teaching of various trades, so that none may live lives of laziness within the Church.

APPENDIX

Appendix D

SOME DOCUMENTS CIRCULATED TO THE CHRISTIAN COUNCIL RELATING TO THE CULT KNOWN AS SERAPHIM

'The herebelow documents were lent ... by the kindness of a Christian at Asanti Akim-Odumasi, through ... (a) Catechist there.
(A) Undated, and in Manuscript: -
GENERAL MESSAGE
Delivered by Holy Gabriel. Through Bro. S ... N ...
at AC 21/1/52
Recorded by Bro. M. K. O... A...
Witnessed by Bro. O ...

i From date of this message no brother or sister should sit on the left hand side of any driver of 4 wheeled prepared vehicle, when he or she is travelling on a wheeled vehicle of this description. Should in the course of the travelling leave a penny in the lorry before dropping from the vehicle to his or her residential area, do this without anyone noticing it. "Danger ahead."

ii The copper ring with Holy Zodiak's sign on it should be carried by every member in the Holy Order without any delay. Bec Zodiac has been empowered to destroy the ungodly from the earth. And we should be very careful of our movements with regards to Morals.

iii Failing to comply with this, will result BAD, said "I am what I am."

There is added at the bottom of the page in another hand: - Please take copy and return this
F. W.K (the last initial is indistinct).

(B). Original, in typescript: -
A copy of a Circular of the Cult called the
Seraphim and Cherubim
Strictly Confidential　　　　　　　　　　　　　Odumasi Temple
Members only　　　　　　　　　　　　　　　16th Dec. 1951
Very Urgent

General Message to All
Each and everyone should try as far as possible to abide
by the following Message
peace be unto thee

1. Three days to the Christmas should be observed as a River Bath Day. All brethren should go to river bath. Everyone must mix the following with his or her pomade and use for seven days:
    A white flower, Incense and sand from the river mixed with olive-oil.
2. From the three days to the Christmas no one must travel.
3. On the Christmas Day, please light the Holy-Michael light on the altar early in the morning and leave it till late in the evening.
4. Nobody should use the front seat of a vehicle whenever one is travelling: as these places are very very dangerous.
5. Before a brother or a sister travels, she or he must ask leave from the God or the Father for him to lead and guide the one during the journey, more especially when travelling

on a vehicle.
6. Wash with the following for seven days: -
   7 Sea Pebbles (Gravels or stones will do)
   3 pieces of Incense and Holy-Water.
7. At Midnight on 31st December 1951, please go to the altar and pray.
8. Our Lodge (Cherubim and Seraphim) should have been more powerful than it is at present, but because of lack of faith it is not. Every brethren is asked by the Father to fast three days. (As his or her strength may determine), during the fasting, do not eat pepper and use Psalm 23 for prayers. Make Holy Trinity Sign with either sea sand or ordinary sand mixed with sea water before your altar and pray on it. Use the Psalm 23.
9. No sister should allow a person who is not a sister to dress or tie her hair for her.
10. Before 1951 ends, all brethren should make their copper ring with Holy Zodiak Sign (- and send to Brother President, Moorso to bless them).

AMEN

From Holy Gabriel per sister D ... of D... and recorded by Bro. A ... T ... of K ...
(C) A carbon copy of Typescript; undated, I understand drawn up by the Presbyterian Church, in connection with a recent Synod, where the Seraphim were condemned, and Presbyterian members, who will not leave the cult were excommunicated, or so I hear.

SERAPHIM CULT

The Seraphim Cult is a mixture of Christianity, Rosicrucianism, Gnosticism and Heathenism. It is believed to have come from Nigeria to this country. The chief centres in the Gold Coast where there are Temples, as their Meeting Places are called, are Accra, Mangoase, Kumasi and Odumasi-Konongo. Membership is open to both Christians and pagans of both sexes. Before a person becomes a member he has to be initiated. This ceremony, which is like a second baptism, takes place at midnight in a neighbouring stream. All worshippers and initiates wear white gowns with flowing sleeves, giving them the appearance of angels. The inside of the Temples is said to be divided into two apartments by a piece of calico. Behind the partition are images of Angels, the Virgin Mary and Jesus Christ.

The main teaching is that members will be able to live up to the standard of holiness of the angels, hence the name Seraphim. A certain old woman who recently denounced the cult told me that she was told, when she joined the cult, that in Heaven there were certain angels who were so much respected by God that whatever they asked Him for men, He would do it. To get favour before God, therefore, a person should befriend one of these respectable angels, who as a mediator would plead in the presence of God for such a person. These angels are called Seraphim. To achieve this aim is to pray or worship through the Seraphim. One of them who is still a leader of the cult here told me that they do not actually worship the angels but they were trying zealously to equal them. They look upon these angels as models for Christian holiness and service to God. For members to possess all the deepest secrets, which are hidden to the uninitiated, for working miracles, for faith-healing and for freeing them from the power of witchcraft, ghosts and bad spirits, they should befriend an angel, fast as often as possible and abstain from meat on certain days of the week. Their doctrine emphasizes asceticism and denial of the sensuous world; they believe fasting is a merit and an end in itself instead of its only being a means to an end. The picture of the Lord Jesus is displayed before the members for them to look on it and weep bitterly over it for forgiveness of their sins.

APPENDIX

Their standing rule is that the practice of the cult should be kept strictly secret; any member divulging it would go mad.

At their prayers they burn incense, light candles, wear the crucifix and put off their sandals from their feet at their prayer-meeting and public prayers.

They aver that any Church that has members who belong to Seraphim is sure to grow spiritually.

The cult is doing a great deal of harm to the Church in Ashanti where most of the Christian members are easily wheedled away from the truth. What is worse is that most of the leaders of the cult are some of our own Catechists and Teachers.

Note on the above:

(i) I have not heard of a Seraphim Temple in Kumasi – there may be one.
(ii) I am of the opinion that they do insist on baptism before membership, and baptism administered by an "orthodox" Christian group.
(iii) While the members are asked to imitate the angels, I understand that there is no renunciation of the married state; while the group is ascetically minded, it seems to be in many ways, but not in that of sex.
(iv) Noticing that there are both sexes in the group, and that some members of either sex seem to be somewhat in power, I am tempted to wonder how "incorporal" the angel they are supposed to befriend really is. I have heard that at times there is gross licence among the members – I do not know how far this rumour is justified, but it is to be noted that in all the papers written out above, there is not one word of sex-moral.

With regard to this last remark, I was once warned by our Church Elders at Odumase Asante – 'Akim to be very careful before baptizing grown-ups as they often seek "Church" baptism only so as to be able to join the Seraphim Cult.'

X.X.

www.ingramcontent.com/pod-product-compliance
Lightning Source LLC
Chambersburg PA
CBHW071359290426
44108CB00014B/1611